TREK

The Unauthorized Story of the

MOVIES

James Van Hise
Hal Schuster

PIONEER BOOKS INC

Recently Released Pioneer Books...

MTV: MUSIC YOU CAN SEE	ISBN#1-55698-355-7
TREK: THE NEXT GENERATION CREW BOOK	ISBN#1-55698-363-8
TREK: THE PRINTED ADVENTURES	ISBN#1-55698-365-5
THE CLASSIC TREK CREW BOOK	ISBN#1-55698-368-9
TREK VS THE NEXT GENERATION	ISBN#1-55698-370-0
TREK: THE NEXT GENERATION TRIBUTE BOOK	ISBN#1-55698-366-2
THE HOLLYWOOD CELEBRITY DEATH BOOK	ISBN#1-55698-369-7
LET'S TALK: AMERICA'S FAVORITE TV TALK SHOW HOSTS	ISBN#1-55698-364-6
HOT-BLOODED DINOSAUR MOVIES	ISBN#1-55698~365-4
BONANZA: THE UNOFFICIAL STORY OF THE PONDEROSA	ISBN#1-55698-359-X
THE KUNG FU BOOK	ISBN#1-55698-328-X
TREK: THE DEEP SPACE CELEBRATION	ISBN#1-55698 330-1
TREK: THE DEEP SPACE CREW BOOK	ISBN#1-55698-335-2
TREK: THE ENCYCLOPEDIA	ISBN#1-55698-331-X

TO ORDER CALL TOLL FREE: (800)444-2524 ext. 67
credit cards happily accepted

Library of Congress Cataloging-in-Publication Data
James Van Hise, 1959—
Hal Schuster, 1955—

Trek: The Unauthorized Story of the Movies

1.   Trek: The Unauthorized Story of the Movies

(television, popular culture)
I. Title

Published by Pioneer Books, Inc., 5715 N. Balsam Rd., Las Vegas, NV, 89130.

First Printing, 1995

PUBLISHER, EDITOR, DESIGNER: Hal Schuster
COVER ART BY Bruce Wood, COVER DESIGN BY Hal Schuster

TABLE OF CONTENTS

TREK
The Unauthorized Story of the
MOVIES

THE STAR TREK REVIVAL

The movies saved STAR TREK. The classic TV series nearly died after the second season, and was cancelled after the third. No live action stories appeared for a decade. Then the movies revived the franchise. The success of the movies gave birth to THE NEXT GENERATION, DEEP SPACE NINE and VOYAGERS.

Many NEXT GENERATION fans came aboard after the struggle to revive STAR TREK. They attended, and even organized, STAR TREK conventions only after the new television series appeared.

STAR TREK: GENERATIONS, the seventh STAR TREK feature film, officially marks the changing of the guard for the big screen. Television now offers four versions of STAR TREK.

Twenty years ago, a revival was just a dream. Most believed it could not be done. No TV series with so little success to its name had ever been reborn.

The combination of hope and despair fans felt working for a revival, month after month, year after year, defies description. Ten years passed between the last television episode of STAR TREK and the rebirth of the series on the big screen.

Fans attended convention after convention listening to Gene Roddenberry and the STAR TREK actors talk of plans for the future. By 1975 STAR TREK conventions often drew between 5,000 and 8,000 people. No other science fiction convention ever achieved this record.

INTRODUCTION

In the early '70s the STAR TREK phenomenon was the subject of an article in TV GUIDE. By the mid-Seventies, when I pitched an idea for an article about STAR TREK to TV GUIDE, the editors believed their coverage had ended; STAR TREK was dead.

Now TV GUIDE runs two or three STAR TREK covers every year, and added a weekly science fiction column. A letter this year complained about their "excessive" coverage of STAR TREK, only to be followed a few weeks later by another special STAR TREK issue.

After the cancellation of the classic series, only animated appeared before 1979. Less than twenty episodes demonstrated to Paramount that the series still had a following.

Science fiction conventions became big business in the mid-Seventies. Even the World Science Fiction Convention and the San Diego Comic Convention drew only small crowds in 1975. Convention attendance swelled with hordes of STAR TREK fans and dealers, encouraging entrepreneurs to launch STAR TREK conventions.

Fans with more enthusiasm than common sense ran conventions. They thought attending a few conventions taught them how to run one. Details they never even knew existed strangled their efforts. James Doohan appeared at one mid-Seventies convention, but, due to mismanaged publicity, few fans attended and the organizers never paid him. Another convention saved money by presenting William Shatner in a hotel room instead of a convention center. Fans crowded in while dealers ran their tables in similar rooms. The two young women who put on the convention met their hero and that was all that mattered to them.

Large conventions also ran into disasters. A woman who staged two extremely successful STAR TREK conventions promised free rooms to volunteers. The volunteers were handed their hotel bills after she left town. A co-chairman of a Florida convention resigned two weeks before the convention, taking hundreds of dollars with him and leaving a trail of unpaid bills.

One convention promoter paid guests and security guards with rubber checks. They started bouncing during the convention, leading to his arrest in the middle of an event. Dealers put up additional money to keep the doors open the following day.

The circus ended.

Now professional promoters run the STAR TREK conventions. Creation holds exclusive personal appearance contracts with the actors, including Leonard Nimoy and William Shatner. They organize annual super-conventions on both coasts and a series of smaller conventions in cities across the country.

STAR TREK became big business in the 1970s. Paramount issued temporary licenses to dealers to make and sell STAR TREK items, including posters, photographs, buttons, and the like. Later Paramount demanded that STAR TREK convention dealers only sell official merchandise.

The QVC shopping channel sells a multitude of official STAR TREK merchandise, but collectors miss the hundreds of photos once found at conventions. Now there are only 80 official photos.

Most fans attend conventions to see their heroes, actors from the original STAR TREK, DEEP SPACE NINE and the NEXT GENERATION. The actors enjoy meeting their fans, signing autographs and answering questions. They learn about their audience. Every major actor has made multiple convention appearances, except for Avery Brooks. His only public appearance came in November of 1993 at Universal Studios.

STAR TREK conventions continue to grow and prosper. They underwent a transition in the late 1980s with the birth of THE NEXT GENERATION. Conventions that featured the original STAR TREK cast for more than ten years gradually supplanted them with the crew of THE NEXT GENERATION.

The original STAR TREK produced 79 TV episodes and six movies; THE NEXT GENERATION has already produced 178 episodes and one feature film. The original STAR TREK actors couldn't compete.

THE NEXT GENERATION replaced the original series in the hearts of fans. Now they are making the leap to the giant screen while DEEP SPACE NINE continues on television, joined by Voyagers. None of the DEEP SPACE NINE cast appeared in STAR TREK: GENERATIONS. They may show up in future NEXT GENERATION films.

STAR TREK outlived the original series. The future lies wide open.

STAR TREK

THE MOTION PICTURE

THE REVIEW

STAR TREK: THE MOTION PICTURE was first released December 7, 1979. Rumors flew that Kirk and the crew met God.

The slow, ponderous movie dwelled on spectacular special effects to the detriment of story and character. The film appeared clinical and dispassionate, too antiseptic to engage emotions.

The home video release is better. Scenes cut from the theatrical release reappeared on video giving each character key moments. For example, Spock wept after his mind meld with V'ger.

The film failed to deliver a STAR TREK experience. Douglas Trumbull cohort Mike Minor devised a better ending rejected by Paramount as too costly. The film was already over budget to meet its December release date.

Director Robert Wise hated his final cut but Paramount forbade re-editing. People at the Washington, DC premiere reported observing Wise burying his face in his hands in obvious embarrassment.

Roddenberry's novelization of the script contained the background material and human interest missing from the film. Added scenes included a semi-retired, San Francisco based Kirk involved with a woman who uses him as a PR gimmick for Starfleet. He spent his time lecturing and dreaming about his space adventures.

His lover died in the transporter accident with Sonak on screen but the movie neglected to tell the audience who she was. It was quite amusing to imagine womanizer Kirk as the playtoy of a powerful woman.

The novel also showed the effect of Ilia's potent sexual chemistry on a physically aroused Sulu. The revealing scene never made it to the screen.

These moments did not reappear in the video release. Even on video, the film remained disappointing, although Gene Roddenberry's brainchild remained his favorite STAR TREK movie.

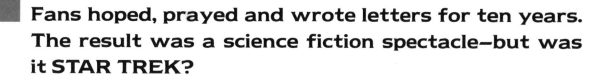

Fans hoped, prayed and wrote letters for ten years. The result was a science fiction spectacle—but was it STAR TREK?

STAR TREK: THE MOTION PICTURE

STAR TREK: THE MOTION PICTURE signaled new life for a defunct television series in 1979. It rose phoenix-like from the ashes, and launched a series of leaps by long-defunct TV series to the big screen. It wasn't greeted with open arms.

Fans wanted STAR TREK back. They began organizing in 1973, after the first convention in New York City. Over the next two years dozens of conventions appeared throughout the country. The defunct TV series sold more merchandise than when it was on the air.

Television loves talking about itself, so the actors and creative people of STAR TREK appeared on many talk shows. THE TOMORROW SHOW, hosted by Tom Snyder, capitalized on interest in STAR TREK. Snyder devoted a special hour to STAR TREK one night in 1975. Walter Koenig, James Doohan, DeForest Kelley and Harlan Ellison appeared as featured guests. They discussed the enduring popularity of STAR TREK and its passionate fans. They also seriously discused a STAR TREK motion picture.

THE MOTION PICTURE

STAR WARS hadn't appeared in theaters yet, but Walter Koenig hit the nail on the head when he observed the pitfalls of bringing a small screen TV show to the big screen. He said, "The only problem is, if [STAR TREK]'s a feature film as opposed to a made-for-television show, they'll decide that they have to change the thrust of it in some way, make it monsters and huge battle scenes; something that you can't get on television. You may distort the entire feeling of the show."

He accurately predicted STAR TREK: THE MOTION PICTURE. The road to the big screen turned long and treacherous as they changed STAR TREK by inches.

Paramount dangled the first carrot in front of starved fans in 1975. They announced a two to three million dollar budget for a STAR TREK film if Gene Roddenberry provided a suitable script.

LIFE AFTER STAR TREK

Gene Roddenberry had mixed feelings. He saw STAR TREK as an albatross around his neck, but it was all he had. His other projects failed after STAR TREK. His 1968 Tarzan screenplay never went before the cameras. His feature film, PRETTY MAIDS ALL IN A ROW, died at the box office. Even his TV Sci Fi, GENESIS II and THE QUESTOR TAPES, pleased fans but failed to satisfy the networks. Science fiction virtually disappeared from television until STAR WARS changed the picture.

Roddenberry had a new son, Eugene, born the year before, and no successes. He needed a job. Heeding Paramount's call, he rewrote the now famous "Enterprise meets God" storyline. Paramount turned it down.

The studio again killed STAR TREK in June of 1977. George Takei believed Paramount never intended to produce a movie. They only wanted free publicity and increased interest in the syndicated classic TV series.

The studio then commissioned a series of ideas from writers. John D. F. Black submitted an outline, as did Theodore Sturgeon, Robert Silverberg and even Ray Bradbury. In one legendary incident Harlan Ellison encountered a dimwitted producer who insisted his story include ancient Mayans. DeForest Kelley said Paramount wanted "JAWS in space."

HIDDEN DISPUTES

Leonard Nimoy released an autobiography in 1975. Some STAR TREK fans found the title, I AM NOT SPOCK, ominous. Nimoy recounted his life and his work, focusing on his relationship with the character that made him famous. In some humorous passages, Nimoy engaged in imaginary conversations with Spock. These illuminated similarities between the actor and the Vulcan.

Nimoy clarified his separate identity from Spock. The book never demeaned Spock or STAR TREK but celebrated the possibilities the series introduced into his life after nearly two decades of struggle.

Nimoy questioned whether he would again play Spock even though he'd performed the voice of Spock for the Filmation

THE MOTION PICTURE

animated series in 1973-74. He now engaged in secret negotiations with Paramount regarding unpaid royalties. No agreement covered the use of his likeness for merchandise.

The issue was a very large thorn in Leonard Nimoy's side by the late Seventies. He refused to play Spock again until they came to terms. Angry fans, unaware of the negotiations, thought Nimoy had turned his back on Spock.

Meanwhile Paramount searched for "the right script." Gene Roddenberry remained hopeful. He discussed his hopes for the feature film in a 1976 wire service interview. He suggested a broader revival of STAR TREK, saying, "I expect that if the feature turns out well, Paramount will try to bring STAR TREK back to television. I would

hope that it would take the form of occasional films in the long form. I don't think I could face the insanity of another weekly STAR TREK."

Paramount abruptly canceled plans for the motion picture in early 1977. They cited the lack of a good script, among other problems. Then STAR WARS reordered science fiction's place in the movie making universe in May of 1977. Paramount wanted a new TV series, to be called STAR TREK II. It would be the cornerstone for a planned new Paramount network.

RODDENBERRY RETURNS

Paramount hired Roddenberry to create the new STAR TREK series in 1977. He dusted off an old GENESIS II story treatment called

"Robot's Return." The story tells of a satellite launched from earth in the late 20th century which returns 250 years later. During its voyage, the satellite gained self-awareness. It now seeks its creator, a being called "NASA."

The story was similar to the original STAR TREK episode, "The Changeling." Roddenberry often reworked old ideas, sometimes simply because he forgot. He turned to science fiction novelist Alan Dean Foster, then busy turning STAR TREK animated scripts into novels, to rewrite "Robot's Return."

Nimoy didn't want any part of STAR TREK II. Spock wouldn't be along for the new voyage. Instead Roddenberry created a new Vulcan character, Lieutenant Xon, briefly known as Lieutenant Vulcan. He became the new Vulcan science officer on the bridge of the Enterprise.

They cast David Gautreaux as Xon. Persis Khambatta signed on to play another new character, the exotic and alluring Ilia. Commodore Decker joined as a third new character.

Nimoy refused to return because of his dispute with Paramount, but he also turned down other series TV offers. Three years on STAR TREK and another two on MISSION: IMPOSSIBLE tired Nimoy out. He no longer wanted to do weekly epsiodic television, and even left MISSION: IMPOSSIBLE a year before his contract expired.

IN THY IMAGE

Alan Dean Foster finished his story treatment, and renamed "Robot's

Will Decker and Indian actress Persis Khambatta as Lieutenant Ilia. Gene Roddenberry believed that a bald-headed woman was incredibly sexy, so the actress shaved her head for the role. Although she prepared herself for the moment when they would shave her beautiful long hair off, she burst into tears when the locks were shed.

Paramount announced the new film at a lavish press conference held on March 28, 1978. The entire cast assembled, including Grace Lee Whitney, who had not appeared in a new STAR TREK story since 1967.

Whitney recently recounted the many ups and downs of her life. After her character was eliminated from the cast of STAR TREK, she had slid into alcoholism and prostitution. Her alco-holism reportedly caused her to be dropped from the cast. She had not completely recovered when she appeared in STAR TREK: THE MOTION PICTURE. Whitney finally, dramatically, turned her life around in the last decade.

She has an important scene in STAR TREK: THE MOTION PICTURE, and made cameo appearances in STAR TREK III: THE SEARCH FOR SPOCK, STAR TREK IV: THE VOYAGE HOME, and STAR TREK VI: THE UNDISCOVERED COUNTRY.

BUDGET WOES

Paramount announced a budget of $15 million for STAR TREK: THE MOTION PICTURE in March 1978; $6 million more than STAR WARS cost. Michael Eisner, then president of Paramount Pictures, stressed the

Return " as "In Thy Image." Roddenberry asked Harold Livingston and Robert Goodwin to turn it into a two-hour teleplay for the premiere episode of STAR TREK II. A dozen additional scripts were completed, including "Kitumba" by John Meredyth Lucas, "Deadlock" by David Ambrose, "Tomorrow and the Stars" by Larry Alexander, "The Savage Syndrome" by Margaret Armen and Alf Harris, "Home" by Worley Thorne, "Devil's Due" by Bill Lansford and "The Child" by John Povill and Jaron Summers. A revised "The Child" was later turned into a script for STAR TREK: THE NEXT GENERATION in 1988.

Plans for Paramount's fourth network hit a snag in the fall of 1977, weeks before shooting was to begin on STAR TREK II. Paramount pulled the plug on November 11, 1977. Contracts were paid off and set construction halted. The studio now planned a feature film instead.

STAR WARS and CLOSE ENCOUNTERS OF THE THIRD KIND proved science fiction packed in theater audiences. STAR TREK: THE MOTION PICTURE went on the drawing board. Paramount signed Robert Wise to helm the project. He had worked on Orson Welles CITIZEN KANE in 1940, and directed THE DAY THE EARTH STOOD STILL in 1951. Many consider the latter film to be the first science fiction movie for adults rather than children. He also directed such hits as WEST SIDE STORY and THE SOUND OF MUSIC.

SUPPORTING PLAYERS

Supporting actors in the movie included newcomers Stephen Collins as

THE MOTION PICTURE

importance of visual effects. It should have been a warning bell.

STAR TREK was not driven by special effects. Strong stories and likable characters brought STAR TREK its audience. Many movie industry executives misunderstood the appeal of STAR WARS. Special effects helped tell the story, but it's success came from dialogue and character development.

Special effects dominated the STAR TREK film from the first. Robert Abel, then head of special effects for STAR TREK: THE MOTION PICTURE, told the trade publication DAILY VARIETY that two-thirds of the picture involved opticals, special effects and animation. Robert Abel won awards for making commercials. His studio was then one of the few set up specifically to do special effects. John Dykstra and Douglas Trumbull were busy with other projects, so Paramount gambled on Abel.

Originally Robert Abel gave Paramount a budget estimate of $4 million for the special effects. The estimate swelled with overruns and problems. Many rewrites drove the price up. Abel's cost estimate hit $16 million by December 1978, a million dollars more than Paramount's announced budget for the whole movie. Paramount grew concerned.

PUTTING ON A GOOD FACE

The September 1978 MILLIMETER magazine featured a glowing profile of Robert Abel and Associates. It hinted that his best work would appear in the STAR TREK movie.

Abel explained his philosophy of filmmaking in the article. He said, "When I was in the cinema department [of UCLA], the message was, 'If you want to send a message, use Western Union, but if you want to make movies, the name of the game is to sell tickets at the box office.'" Abel changed his tune after watching Stanley Kubrick's 2001: A SPACE ODYSSEY, which depended on spectacular visuals. The final version of STAR TREK: THE MOTION PICTURE owes more to that film than STAR WARS.

Abel explained, "Kubrick proved you can make an art film and make money at the box office. It was, in its realm of special effects, the breakthrough that CITIZEN KANE was to the live action film. It was a milestone." Abel forgot that the expensive 2001: A SPACE ODYSSEY took seven years to break even. It was not a commercial hit.

Jeffrey Altshuler, executive producer for Robert Abel and Associates, understood this misguided interpretation of the importance of visual effects. He told MILLIMETER, "The film (2001: A SPACE ODYSSEY) took away the basic narrative and substituted terrific visuals. It made the viewer more open to visual images and that affects the kind of work that comes out of here. A lot of the work is strictly a visual message." Sadly, the philosophy of Robert Abel and Associates remained to plague the production after they left.

Paramount had turned all of their models and other work over to their special effects division, Magicam, when

STAR TREK II was canceled. Magicam had worked on the original model of V'ger for "In Thy Image." The motion picture needed new props with additional detail. The fourteen foot V'ger would go through many changes.

The Robert Abel Group envisioned photographing the model with a twenty-one inch model of the Enterprise to establish scale. Douglas Trumbull later chose a 70 kilometer model.

CLASHES WITH MAGICAM

Magicam always wanted to do the special effects for STAR TREK: THE MOTION PICTURE. They considered it a slap in the face when Paramount went with a larger, outside house. Subcontractors said the staff became belligerent and difficult to work with.

Brick Price recounted delivering a model to Magicam only to have the door slammed in his face.

Designer Andrew Probert visited Magicam while the new Klingon ship was being built. He pointed out a flaw in the model. Magicam refused to correct it. When it came time to shoot, they had to correct it. Probert found Magicam difficult and unfriendly.

Richard Taylor took charge when Robert Abel & Associates took over the special effects. Magicam made some of the models seen on screen, including the space dock surrounding the Enterprise when it first appears early in the film. They built the space dock with half inch glass tubing bent into shapes by an aerospace tube bender facility. The tubing supported thousands of wires. The space dock took five months to complete and included fifty-six neon grids. The six by six inch grids each required three thousand volts of electricity to operate. Each neon panel had its own transformer and huge cables.

Magicam effects appeared in key sequences, including the Enterprise in dry-dock, the Vulcan shuttle and all the travel pods and work bees in the dry-dock sequence. Miniatures were used of the Enterprise in dry-dock for some scenes, while in others the dry-dock was matted over the Enterprise to obtain adequate depth of field.

ABEL ON THE OUTS

The swelling budget and conflicts with Magicam forced Paramount to drop the Robert Abel Group. Brick Price blamed the falling out on the studio's constant reshooting of footage. He dismissed published reports that Abel was fired after director Robert Wise requested a screening of completed footage in December of 1978 and was shown a minute and a half of film. Studio politics played a role in Abel's firing. Abel never discussed his side of the dispute, although he sued NEW WEST magazine for their coverage. Abel and Paramount ended their relationship on February 22, 1979.

Robert Wise tried to be diplomatic. He said, "I want simply to say that they were very creative people and they had excellent ideas, but the big concern that we had was whether they would be able to execute all of the effects in time so the film would be ready for its release date of December 7. That was what made us decide [to make] the change.

"It wasn't lack of creativeness or abilities or anything like that. They were very good, had very good ideas, but I don't think they were equipped yet to execute fast enough such a big amount of very sophisticated effects. That was a giant picture in terms of effects and work involved."

Douglas Trumbull saw signs of trouble as early as August of 1978. He offered to work with the studio after his commitments finished on other projects. Paramount turned him down. They later took him up on his offer, first as a consultant in January of 1979, then as head of special effects in March.

THE SPACE ODYSSEY

Douglas Trumbull had ound fame on Stanley Kubrick's 2001: A SPACE ODYSSEY. He later wrote and directed the cult science fiction classic SILENT RUNNING and created the special effects for CLOSE ENCOUNTERS OF THE THIRD KIND. After STAR TREK: THE MOTION PICTURE, he worked on BLADE RUNNER, BRAINSTORM (which he directed) and other major motion pictures. Recently he has designed elaborate amusement park rides. His most famous are the BACK TO THE FUTURE ride at Universal Studios and his Showscan production for the Luxor in Las Vegas.

Trumbull and the studio faced a dilemma on STAR TREK: THE MOTION PICTURE. The film was already months behind schedule. Theaters post advance bonds to secure a film. If a film is postponed, the theater can cancel the contract and request a refund. Paramount didn't want to return money. They had to make their promised delivery date even if it required overtime by all of the special effects houses.

Trumbull inherited the work from the Robert Abel Group. He admired their plans but felt they couldn't do the storyboarded visuals in time. None of the Robert Abel Group's final optical effects made it into the film. Some live action special effects shot by Abel's crew appeared as the glowing V'ger probe on the bridge.

THE MAJOR PROBLEM

Director Robert Wise headed the live action filming. Ordinarily a director hires cast and crew. The primary cast for STAR TREK had been in place for over a decade. Wise noted, "I came into a situation that was already set in many ways. That's very unusual for me. I'd never worked this way before, and it was kind of a strange feeling. I'm learning to deal with it, finding ways in which I can alter things that have already been set. Since I couldn't start from scratch I've tried to upgrade things and improve them so they'll all come out looking like they belong in the same film."

The director said time was his biggest problem. Wise explained, "The challenge of doing the effects and getting them up there and dealing with them is no problem for me. The time I have to do them in, that everybody

THE MOTION PICTURE

has to do them in, is the problem.

"I want to make one point that is very important. There is nothing more important on any film than the foreground, the actors, the story. That's what we worked on like a son-of-a-gun. We had to be sure that the story we put in front of these marvelous photographic effects was going to be worthy of them and hopefully hold its own against the special photographic effects and not suffer by comparison."

Wise convinced Paramount to hire Leonard Nimoy. Nimoy was still fighting with Paramount over unpaid royalties. Paramount refused to compromise. Finally, days before the March 28, 1978, press conference, Wise persuaded the studio to settle. Paramount relented. The ink was barely dry on Nimoy's contract when he appeared before the press with the rest of the cast. It was later reported that Paramount paid Nimoy $2.5 million, including his fee for acting in STAR TREK: THE MOTION PICTURE.

CASTING STAR TREK

Wise told ENTER-PRISE magazine (September, 1978), "The only person that I was involved with in casting was Stephen Collins, who played Decker, because even Persis Khambatta had been set. They had the original team of special effects men already at work and a number of the sets were already done.

"There is one area that I did have influence on: I upgraded the sets considerably from what they had originally built. What you saw in the film

is not at all what I came on to. We did a lot of improvements on the Bridge set, we threw away their corridors and built those you saw. We redesigned the engine room entirely — in fact there was nothing left of the original engine room, just the superstructure. The interior of the ship was changed considerably according to my indications."

The screenplay had already passed through many hands when Wise was hired. Harold Livingston is the writer of record, but producer Gene Roddenberry did his own rewriting, causing a variety of problems, most notably for the director.

Wise said, "It was one of those situations where we started with an incomplete script — we knew the story, of course, but the actual final parts of the script were being worked on constantly as we were shooting! I think that when we started early in 1978, we only had the first act of the script. From there on we were changing and rewriting. I had some influence on the first act, and tried to have as much as I could on the rest of the film, but it is a very sloppy way to make a film."

PORTRAYING THE CREW

Wise brought new ideas to the production, including capitalizing on the large crew of the spaceship. "The good thing about doing a film," Wise said, "is that for the first time we can have a visual perspective you can't get in television. We'll see the tremendous size of the Enterprise. In the series, where they said there were 430 crew members, we're going to show them all."

He set out to do it with the help of droves of STAR TREK fans. It was Gene Roddenberry's way of thanking them. They would work from one to two days for $75 a day.

Bjo Trimble had helped organize the save STAR TREK writing campaign in 1967-68. She now helped contact fans to appear in the film. The Paramount casting office stipulated that the fans had to be at least 20 but no older than 40. The women must be between 5'6" and 5'8" and could wear size 8 to 10. The men could be from 5'8" to 6'2" and had to fit into size 40 to 42 garments. Exceptions were made for people who appeared in the crowd scene in the Rec Room since Bjo Trimble was shorter than 5'6," as was the wife of director Robert Wise.

Roddenberry avoided appearing at the casting call so he didn't have to deal with rejected fans. Only a few could be chosen. Every costume had an emblem identifying the crew member's "duty" on the Enterprise. Some fans got to be aliens. One fan chosen was the now adult son of actress Grace Lee Whitney. The boy had also been an extra in the original STAR TREK episode "Miri."

APPLAUDING WINNERS

A loophole in the contract with the Extras Guild allowed non-Guild members to be hired after enough Guild members had been employed for that day. The Guild extras found it strange that fans applauded every time someone was chosen, even though some applauding fans had already been rejected.

Fans reported at the studio at 7 AM for make up for the day of shooting. Filming began at 1 PM, right after lunch. They completed the shots that day by going into overtime, avoiding having to return hundreds of people to be dressed and made up again the following morning.

Special effects for the giant view screen on the Enterprise would be added later. Robert Wise assembled his multitude in the Rec Room to see slides representing the missing special effects. Some crew members on the Enterprise watched family members die when Epsilon 9 was destroyed by V'ger. The extras were supposed to react solemnly to what they "saw" transpiring on the large view screen.

Wise gave the group directons, including, "Now you see the enemy strike again. It's awesome. You're horrified! You can't believe it! React!"

They shot short takes with different angles of the same scene. Two minutes on screen took the rest of the day to shoot. Fans searched crowd scenes for familiar faces after the film appeared on video.

The ambitious scene contained a major error. Robert Wise placed some fans on a balcony overlooking the Rec Room to fill the huge set. This group obscured the large viewports which looked out on a $30,000 diorama depicting the nacelles of the Enterprise and part of the rear of the vessel in space. The artistry is never seen in the film.

THE SPACE WALK

They changed an interesting scene planned for the climax. When Kirk,

THE MOTION PICTURE

Spock and McCoy left the Enterprise, they were to walk across a field of hexagonal cubes. The cubes lit up when they were stepped on. The test footage looked good, but Richard Kline, the cameraman, didn't think it would work, so the cubes remained cold and gray. It resulted in a boring scene Robert Wise cut from the film.

The new head of special effects, Douglas Trumbull, worked with live action shooting that later included special effects, including Spock's spacewalk into V'ger. Originally Spock left the Enterprise, encountered a "Memory Wall," and saved Kirk from V'ger's anti-bodies. The sequence appeared in Gene Roddenberry's novelization of the film. Trumbull came on to the project after they filmed the live action. He knew it would take half the special effects budget to finish it, and finally persuaded Paramount to scrap the footage and write off $380 thousand in sets.

Trumbull delivered a faster paced spacewalk. It didn't involve Kirk. Spock mind-melded with V'ger and was blasted back to the Enterprise.

A section of the original version appeared in the home videotape of STAR TREK:THE MOTION PICTURE when Kirk exited the Enterprise to retrieve Spock's unconscious body. Kirk exited wearing one spacesuit but encountered Spock while wearing a different one. The wooden rafters in the roof of the sound stage were clearly visible when Kirk descended from the Enterprise through the opening above him. The visible parts of the sound stage would have been covered with matte paintings had the sequence not been abandoned.

Greg Jein's model makers built the planets and other things seen by Spock as he cruised through V'ger with his rocketpack. Jein's unit built the interior of V'ger based on preproduction paintings by Syd Mead rendered late in the film's production.

INSIDE V'GER

Trumbull disliked Syd Mead's art for the maw, the Enterprise's gateway to V'ger. He hadn't liked the representations by other artists either.

Ron Resch finally designed a series of six double-ended cones faceted and interlocked with a hexagonal orifice that irised open. Drawings couldn't convey the unusual design to the special effects team. Resch constructed a three-dimensional model.

The two-dimensional motion picture lost the complexities of the design. Only the rhythmic opening and closing of the iris remained.

Veteran science fiction artist Bob McCall visualized Spock's spacewalk. He had painted four publicity posters for 2001: A SPACE ODYSSEY in 1968, and produced concept paintings in 1971 for a never produced TV version of THE WAR OF THE WORLDS and later for the 1980 film THE BLACK HOLE. Several of his paintings for STAR TREK: THE MOTION PICTURE appear in his book, VISION OF THE FUTURE: THE ART OF ROBERT McCALL (Harry N. Abrams, Inc. Publishers, 1982).

McCall painted the large image of Ilia floating inside V'ger by making a plaster cast of the head and shoulders of actress Persis Khambatta. He attached it to a mannequin and shot it with proper lighting. They made and retouched 16 x 20 prints later shot on an animation stand. The energy globe on her neck is the center of attention. They added movement when it was shot, cheaply creating the look of a much more complicated effect.

BUILDING THE ENTERPRISE

They raced to beat the clock, hiring every available special effects professional to work twenty-four hours a day. Trumbull took full control in March 1979. The film had to be finished by early November to be delivered to theaters by December 7. That it was Pearl Harbor Day didn't escape the notice of Paramount.

Trumbull had hired John Dykstra's Apogee, the facility he established after his falling out with George Lucas. Trumbull also reassembled the team of craftsmen he'd just finished working with on CLOSE ENCOUNTERS OF THE THIRD KIND. Magicam built the new version of the Enterprise, restyled by Andrew Probert, based on preliminary designs Joe Jennings had done for the unrealized STAR TREK II. Trumbull and his people completed nearly five hundred special effects cuts in the final nine months of production.

Lee Ettleman of Magicam built the Enterprise around an high strength aluminum armature. The rigid model didn't flex at key pressure points, and supported itself even when mounted at an angle to be photographed. A shell was added and lights installed. Neon tubing for the lights was installed inside the saucer portion. Neon lasts thousands of hours and generates very low levels of heat, important because the saucer wouldn't be opened again. It also wouldn't harm the plastic hull which encased it. Stresses on the model were so great that if the saucer section were opened, it would be impossible to seal it again.

Magicam built too small a model of the Enterprise. They needed a larger one for additional detailing. It wasn't built.

The seven foot long model of the Enterprise was extremely heavy. It required several men to move it into position for photography. This didn't present serious problems to Trumbull. He moved his camera instead of the model. It would later present problems to Industrial Light & Magic on STAR TREK II and STAR TREK III.

THE BLACK SCREEN

STAR TREK: THE MOTION PICTURE used Douglas Trumbull's "black screen" techniques to shoot the Enterprise. Individual detail panels on the surface of the model didn't create lighting problems. ILM later found that those panels reflected light from their blue screen, causing "holes" to appear in the film.

Trumbull filmed the Enterprise with back-lighting rather than traditional front lighting. No light fell on the model itself, leaving it black. They made a print from the matte, loaded it into an Oxberry animation camera and used the camera to project the image on the animation table.

THE MOTION PICTURE

They then used the print as reference.

This form of rotoscoping is combined with a negative of the matte to block out unwanted areas. A matte masks a portion of a photographic image to add special effects such as the view screen on the Enterprise bridge or the transporter sparkle in the old TV series. The matte technique allowed them to combine the Enterprise with the final background for STAR TREK: THE MOTION PICTURE.

An obvious special effect in the film involves the Travel Pod. Like a good magician's trick, how a special effect is achieved should never be obvious. It's obvious that a separate piece of film was combined with the miniature model of the Pod. The footage was rear-projected on a screen in the Travel Pod. Blowing the 35mm live action footage up to 65mm for the special effects footage caused a grainy look. There was no time to fix the problem.

The spectacular opening scene, when three Klingon warships encounter the V'ger cloud, raised audience expectations for more exciting sequences to follow. It never happened. Apogee created the dynamic opening.

IMAGINATIVE EFFECTS

John Dykstra headed three Klingon vessels towards the camera, then rolled the camera and tilted it upwards to view the ships traveling past into the V'ger cloud. They built only one Klingon ship model, photographed it three times, then composited the images. This sequence employed many clever techniques, including photon torpedoes filmed by reflecting a laser beam off a revolving crystal.

They added the cloud to the scene in the final two weeks of production. All Apogee effects were approved by both Douglas Trumbull and Robert Wise. Wise suggested that the Klingon ships move slowly to convey a sense of size and weight.

Filming the spectacular destruction of the three Klingon vessels was complicated. Trumbull suggested that Apogee avoid blowing up the Klingon ships. He wanted something different. They chose an energy burst that flowed up the length of the vessel and consumed it. It represented how V'ger digitized something for electronic storage, although it was never explained in the film.

They wrapped the Klingon ship in aluminum foil and carefully scanned it with a laser. Light reflected from the metal foil in visually interesting ways. They shot from the same angle as existing footage of the models. Later they composited it creating the look of a vessel awash in energy. Then they added the bolts.

Trumbull persuaded the production designers to build a Klingon bridge reminiscent of the cramped confines of an old submarine. Andrew Probert designed the set constructed under the supervision of John Vallone. They built six layers of the model. As V'ger assimilated the ship, they replaced individual layers with blue screens. The digitizing seemed to sweep towards the camera, a section at a time.

They later added the disintegration effects in place of the blue screens. The live action footage was shot specifically with post-production special effects in mind. Sequenced light sources concealed behind each section of the set tie in with later special effects. The last level of blue screen showed the Klingons turning to witness the effect as it engulfed them. It happened quickly on screen.

MATTE PAINTINGS

Matte paintings, usually on glass and illuminated from behind, created memorable special effects for the original STAR TREK series. The paintings of extraterrestrial scenes merged with live action elements or just appeared as an establishing shot. The paintings appeared in the episodes "Where No Man Has Gone Before" (the Lithium Cracking Station), "The Menagerie" (the castle), "Devil In The Dark" (the underground mining facility), "Court Martial" (the cityscape) and "A Taste of Armageddon" (the surface of Eminiar VII). The spectacular images established a sense of other worldly vistas.

STAR TREK: THE MOTION PICTURE used the same technique. The shuttle carrying Capt. Kirk zooms in over the Golden Gate Bridge in the opening sequence. This scene began with Matthew Yuricich painting a futuristic version of the bridge based on a contemporary photo. The cityscape behind the bridge was altered to reflect the three hundred year passage of time, with only the Coit Tower and the Transamerica Building serving as reference points for 20th Century audiences.

Veteran filmmaker Robert Wise was

unaware of the limitations of matte paintings. He asked Matthew Yuricich to paint a matte for the camera to go around the corner of a building. At the time, this could then only be done with a miniature. Now computer modeling programs allow filmmakers to create such effects.

WARP SPECTACULAR

The establishing shot of the tram station as Kirk's tram car arrives is a complicated optical. A floor set was built on a Paramount sound stage with various actors at floor level. A large hanging foreground piece with people appears for scale. The rest of the scene is a matte painting except for the moving air tram, which is a model shot added later.

The tram cast a shadow on the wall to appear to be in the scene. This took time to perfect. The tram car in flight was a miniature. As it passed behind columns in the tram station at Star Fleet Headquarters, it was replaced with the full sized model. They had to precisely match the speed of the model with the speed of the mock-up to create a seamless transition.

Paintings provided the illusion of size and depth in the engine room set. The filmmakers painted a backdrop to create perspective, and laid a perspective painting on the set floor to provide the illusion of additional stories. They then squeezed the area beyond the foreground by using a forced perspective painting as well as dwarfs and children in uniforms.

Trumbull wanted something interesting for the climax. He used the shot of the Enterprise moving past the camera and suddenly stretching as it entered warp. This new portrayal of the Enterprise entering warp has since been copied and reused in subsequent films, as well as, with alterations, in THE NEXT GENERATION. It set the standard.

EXPENSIVE UNDERTAKING

Leonard Nimoy said that the success of STAR WARS led to STAR TREK: THE MOTION PICTURE. STAR WARS also pushed special effects as the centerpiece of the film. An actor resents seeing a technical effect treated as equal to his own contribution. It is demeaning.

Nimoy said, "In STAR TREK: THE MOTION PICTURE we spent a lot of time staring at the view screen on which later would be a lot of sizable special effects. So the climate was problematic.

"I think it was a tastefully presented and produced film; obviously a very well crafted film. Certainly Paramount showed that they were serious about making as fine a picture as possible. They bit the bullet financially. We started out with a $15 million budget and let it expand, hoping for the best."

Its $45 million budget made it the most expensive film until that time. Paramount was not happy.

Paramount made another bad decision during production of the film. They wanted a "G" rating, without realizing that a "G" rating repels part of the movie-going audience. George Lucas chose a stronger rating rather than cutting a handful of frames to secure a "G."

The only "G" rated block-busters are Disney animated features.

THE TRUMBULL ENDING

A rumor of "The Douglas Trumbull ending" spread after ST:TMP was released. The late Mike Minor, a talented artist and technician, had been involved with STAR TREK beginning with the third season of the original TV series. Mike explained that an ending had been abandoned for reasons of time. He had come up with the ending. Trumbull liked it, but felt they didn't have enough time until the delivery date. Greg Jein explained that his shop worked 24 hours a day during the final weeks of production.

This proposed ending, according to Mike Minor, showed the Enterprise ejected by the evolving V'ger, then followed by the three Klingon ships from the opening of the film. When the Klingons woke from stasis they found themselves orbiting the Federation's home-world and began blasting away. The Enterprise defeated the Klingon ships, but was almost destroyed, forcing an evacuation by saucer separation.

Saucer-separation wasn't a new idea when it appeared in the NEXT GENERATION episode "Encounter At Farpoint," but had been discussed for years. This would also have required adding a scene showing the Enterprise being reconstructed in orbit.

, Robert Wise couldn't make the final cuts he wanted on the film because of time constraints. The boring journey through V'ger was among the scenes Wise

THE MOTION PICTURE

wanted to edit to fix the pacing.

RESTORATION

Many changes were made later when the movie aired on ABC. They added twelve minutes of additional character scenes. It made for a better film.

Restored character scenes involved the supporting cast. For instance, after Kirk reported to the bridge of the Enterprise and left to find Will Decker in engineering, Sulu exclaimed, "He wanted her back; he got her!" Uhura responded, "Our chances of returning may have just doubled." It's a small bit, but it adds a flavor of the old STAR TREK and further demonstrated that these people were old friends.

Another scene involved Sulu's reaction to Ilia when she came onto the bridge. In the restored scene, Ilia further explained the reference to her celibacy. She said she never took advantage of a "sexually immature species." Looking at an obviously flustered Sulu, she added, "I'm sworn to celibacy. That makes me as safe as any human female." Sulu never said a word, but the scene is as much his as Ilia's.

More character scenes appeared, including an interesting lingering shot of Ilia on the bridge after Decker left with Kirk and McCoy following the wormhole incident. It's clear that she's worried.

When McCoy questioned whether Spock's presence aboard the Enterprise was purely unselfish, Kirk replied that he could never believe that of Spock. McCoy responded with the disturbing rejoinder, "Jim, how do we know about any of us?" This added to the undercurrent of doubt and complicated emotions in the story.

One restored character line clearly came from Roddenberry. It featured Dr. McCoy discussing V'ger looking for its creator on earth. It believed its creator to be a machine. McCoy remarked that, "We all create God in our own image." It's a thoughtful character line.

A restored scene was one of the best Spock scenes in the history of Trek. On the bridge, Spock turned to Kirk with a tear in the Vulcan's eye, and stated, "I weep for V'ger as I would for a brother. As I was when I came aboard, so V'ger is now — empty, incomplete, searching. Logic and knowledge are not enough." This dovetails with Spock in the Sick Bay scene perfectly, amplifying his character.

Director Robert Wise credited Nimoy with having Spock reveal emotion. He said, "He wanted to give the character more depth. You know, characters are not static; they change, they evolve. I think Leonard was very conscious of this and didn't want to simply repeat his role in the same way as the TV version."

THE NEW VERSION

This version of STAR TREK: THE MOTION PICTURE may still have a wobbly story, but the characters are complete. The film is better and the viewing experience is richer.

The movie released in December 1979 was shaped by several forces. One was scheduling problems, but there were others. Leonard Nimoy disliked working on STAR TREK: THE MOTION PIC-

TURE. He said the writers and directing talent were utterly humorless. The banter Spock and McCoy regularly had on the TV show was utterly absent from the film.

"The feeling was that that was the kind of campy stuff that you did on television but you didn't do it in a movie," Nimoy recalled, giving an example of the thinking. "At the very end of STAR TREK: THE MOTION PICTURE, on the last day of shooting, we were on the bridge of the Enterprise shooting the final scene. Kirk is addressing the rest of the characters who had been gathered for this mission and is offering to return them to where they had been picked up. I'm supposed to say, 'My work on Vulcan is finished.' In the final rehearsal, when McCoy says, 'I'm here, I might as well stay,' and then Kirk turns to me and says, 'I'll have you back on Vulcan in a couple days,' I said, 'If Dr. McCoy is to remain on board, my presence here will be essential.' You won't see that in the movie. It was not allowed.

"There was a very fast conference of all the gray heads and they said, no, it doesn't seem appropriate, people have died and this is a very serious movie. We've come a long way since then. We've learned the value of the laughter and it was one of the wonderful ingredients of the series."

A REASSESSMENT

The film is very different than the six films which followed. The best motion pictures present entertainment larger and richer than television. Hollywood introduced the wide-screen cinemascope in the early 1950s when television made inroads into American life. STAR TREK: THE MOTION PICTURE, under the direction of the old showman Robert Wise, is one of the last such extravaganzas.

That reportedly $45 million budget for ST:TMP was inflated a bit. It didn't only include money spent making the film. It also included all the money Paramount spent trying to revive STAR TREK, including expenditures for the aborted STAR TREK II television series, canceled only after sets were built and contracts were signed. Everyone had to be paid off when the project was canceled. All of this was absorbed into the budget of STAR TREK:THE MOTION PICTURE.

Now movie makers keep one eye on the weekly grosses and the other on the home video market. It wasn't unusual for movies to play in theaters for many months in 1979, or even have a major rerelease. That doesn't happen often any more. It is now rare to see a film made to take full advantage of the wide screen theatrical experience. Only two recent films made this attempt, DIEHARD and JURASSIC PARK.

Many STAR TREK fans never saw STAR TREK: THE MOTION PICTURE on the big screen. It offered a powerful effect. The sequels are superior films, but for sheer spectacle, STAR TREK: THE MOTION PICTURE remains a singular experience.

STAR TREK 2

THE WRATH OF KHAN

THE REVIEW

STAR TREK II: THE WRATH OF KHAN was the first good STAR TREK film. It delivered an engaging plot, plenty of action, a powerful nemesis, dramatic relationships and a famous controversy.

Fans knew Spock would die. They weren't happy. Neither was Gene Roddenberry. Roddenberry quickly learned that a consultant holds no power. The inventor of Spock thought he should have a voice in his fate. Paramount, the producers and the director of THE WRATH OF KHAN overruled him.

The film proved more optimistic than expected, even poking fun at audience expectations. Spock appeared to die in the opening scene at Starfleet Academy. The scene introduced the Kobyashi Maru no-win situation, a very controversial idea among fans, particularly since Kirk cheated to become the only one to ever beat it.

The no-win scenario underlied the rest of the movie. Khan killed people, first the scientists, then Enterprise crew members, including Scotty's nephew, and, finally, Spock. Kirk barely escaped a similar fate.

The film pit Kirk against Khan, although they never met face to face. Paramount's television division shot the film to ensure a six month schedule. The film looked great.

The new uniforms looked better than the boring pastels of the first film, but they're a bad idea. Roddenberry's Starfleet may have the trappings of a quasi-military organization but it's an exploration and peacekeeping force. The uniforms looked as if they belonged on soldiers.

THE WRATH OF KHAN ended with a spectacular space battle. Impressive special effects by Industrial Light & Magic brought it to life.

Spock's dramatic death worked. When his friend Kirk intoned, "You have been, and always will be, my friend," it tugged at audience heartstrings. The end of the very dark film suggested infinite future possibilities.

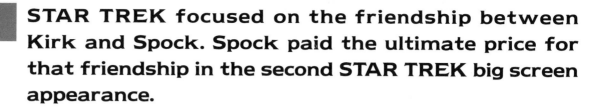

STAR TREK focused on the friendship between Kirk and Spock. Spock paid the ultimate price for that friendship in the second STAR TREK big screen appearance.

STAR TREK II: THE WRATH OF KHAN

STAR TREK: THE MOTION PICTURE received mixed reviews in 1979. It still grossed more than $100 million, but Paramount wasn't happy. They knew they could have kept more of the box office if the film had come in on budget. STAR TREK: THE MOTION PICTURE, at $45 million, was the most expensive film made until that time. Paramount blamed the cost overruns on inefficiency, and Gene Roddenberry.

Roddenberry began writing a sequel when STAR TREK: THE MOTION PICTURE hit the screens. By July 1980 he had finished the script and turned it in to the studio. They rejected it, closed Roddenberry's office on the Paramount lot, and canceled plans for another STAR TREK film.

After the dust had settled by 1981, Paramount tried again, without Roddenberry. They brought in Harve Bennett, an original Hollywood "Quiz Kid," from the early game show, and later producer of popular television fare including THE MOD SQUAD, THE SIX MILLION DOLLAR MAN, THE BIONIC WOMAN and the mini-series RICH MAN,

POOR MAN. Paramount wanted experience. They found it in Bennett.

Gulf & Western chief Charles Bludhorn and production head Barry Diller interviewed Bennett. They asked him what he thought of STAR TREK: THE MOTION PICTURE. He said it ran too long and too dull. Bludhorn wanted to know if Bennett could do cheaper. Bennett replied, "Where I come from, I can make four movies for that."

A RELUCTANT SPOCK

Nimoy told US MAGAZINE that his experience on STAR TREK: THE MOTION PICTURE was not a pleasant one. The legendary Robert Wise didn't get along with his cast. Wise may have resented not choosing his actors, and their questioning his familiarity with their characters. Directors enjoy authority.

Nimoy discussed the options with Paramount., and finally agreed to return. Although he later denied that Spock's death was his idea, Roddenberry said it was in a talk in 1987. The truth lies somewhere in between. Nimoy says Roddenberry spread the story because he hadn't backed Roddenberry against Paramount before the film began. After STAR TREK II: THE WRATH OF KHAN finished filming, Shatner told FANTASTIC FILMS that Nimoy had expressed misgivings about killing the character after he'd worked on the film for several weeks. Nimoy told Shatner he wanted to come back for another film.

The fans besieged Paramount with letters and took out ads, but the studio regarded it as free publicity. It created a heightened sense of anticipation for the film.

Recently Nimoy again denied that Spock's death was his idea, but he certainly didn't oppose it.

TELEVISION FILMMAKING

Harve Bennett wanted to make his film on time and under budget. He used the TV production division to keep costs down to $13 million, even less than Paramount's original announced figure for STAR TREK: THE MOTION PICTURE in 1978.

Bennett wasn't a STAR TREK fan. A former girlfriend had been a big fan and he'd often watched episodes with her.

When shooting began on STAR TREK II: THE WRATH OF KHAN, they found the one piece bridge of the Enterprise. It was difficult to film with a moving camera. Director of Photography for ST:TMP, Richard H. Kline, had requested the bridge be assembled in this manner. He preferred a closed set to moving walls, believing that moving walls hurt credibility. Kline believed actors reacted more realistically to solid walls. He suspended a camera from a monorail in the ceiling to deal with the limited camera angles.

They pulled the bridge apart into detachable sections for STAR TREK II. The new bridge unlocked and rolled out of the way for the camera.

BENNETT'S BACKGROUND

Bennett had never worked with

Roddenberry, but he had worked with Gene Coon in the early '70s. Roddenberry never publicly gave his opinion of Harve Bennett, the man who took his place. He was dismayed at Bennett's casual dismissal of STAR TREK: THE MOTION PICTURE as dull and boring.

Bennett screened several episodes of the original TV series to learn STAR TREK. He stopped after watching "Space Seed." Khan was the perfect villain for his film.

STAR TREK II deals with aging. Kirk wears reading glasses. Bennett and Shatner were the same age. The producer seemed self-conscious of aging. He had married a young woman in her twenties, and became annoyed when an interviewer mistook her for his daughter.

The announced the film as STAR TREK II: THE VENGEANCE OF KHAN, then changed it when George Lucas shot his third STAR WARS film in 1982. Lucas announced his film as THE REVENGE OF THE JEDI. Paramount changed their title to THE WRATH OF KHAN. Then Lucas changed his title to THE RETURN OF THE JEDI. He later claimed never to have called his film REVENGE OF THE JEDI.

CRAFTING CONCEPT

Bennett wrote the story outline for THE WRATH OF KHAN, while Jack B. Sowards wrote the screenplay. Bennett included Khan and Kirk's son, David. Designer Mike Minor added The Genesis Device, and Bennett and Sowards worked it into the storyline. Walter Koenig said Spock originally died halfway through the film, but he suggested it be moved to the climax.

Bennett later added scenes for the supporting actors. George Takei refused to sign until he had at least one good scene. In his 1994 autobiography, TO THE STARS, the actor insists Shatner sabotaged the scene by giving an indifferent performance, forcing the director to leave it on the cutting room floor. Takei never forgave Shatner.

THE LOST SCENE

Although Takei never publicly mentioned this incident before his book, the scene appeared in the revised final draft for STAR TREK II, dated January 18, 1982. It was scene 28 & 29, and took place right after the stolen Reliant arrived at Regula One:

28 EXT. ORBITING SPACE DOCK AREA - TERRA (FEATURE STOCK)

A SPACE SHUTTLE moving toward us.

29 INT. SPACE SHUTTLE

A new composite. Bones, Sulu, Uhura and Kirk — who sits, reading. Through the windows we can see the approach to the starship ENTERPRISE. Kirk looks up, nods. Sulu activates a comm button.

    SULU
Enterprise, this is Admiral Kirk's party on final approach.

    ENT. VOICE
  (filtered)
Enterprise welcomes you. Prepare for docking.

Kirk looks up from his book as Sulu sits next to him.

    KIRK
I really must thank you.

THE WRATH OF KHAN

SULU
(embarrassed)
I am delighted; any chance to go aboard Enterprise, however briefly, is always an excuse for nostalgia.

KIRK
I cut your new orders personally. By the end of the month, you'll have your first command: USS EXCELSIOR.

SULU
Thank you, sir. I've looked forward to this for a long time.

KIRK
You've earned it. But I'm still grateful to have you at the helm for three weeks. I don't believe these kids can steer.

Sulu laughs.

It was Takei's only effective scene in the film. Sulu's promotion to captaincy of the Excelsior finally took place in STAR TREK VI, when Nick Meyer returned as director. Those scenes were filmed without Shatner in the room and were crucial to the plot.

In a recent interview, Shatner insisted that he didn't sabotage the scene, but had questioned Takei's decision to transfer his character off the Enterprise removing Sulu from subsequent films. Shatner had a point. STAR TREK VI: THE UNDISCOVERED COUNTRY jumped through hoops to include Sulu. This wouldn't have been possible for STAR TREK III, IV and V due to the demands of the story.

THE NEW DIRECTOR

Paramount hired director Nicholas Meyer on the strength of one film, TIME AFTER TIME. That film carefully balanced plot and character development. The first time director demonstrated a knack for drama and pacing.

Meyer was born in 1945. He became involved in the film industry after writing LOVE STORY in 1971. His first novel, THE SEVEN PERCENT SOLUTION, became a best-seller. His other novels include TARGET PRACTICE (1974), THE WEST END HORROR (1976), BLACK ORCHID (1977, with Barry Jay Kaplan) and CONFESSIONS OF A HOMING PIGEON (1981). Before TIME AFTER TIME, Meyer wrote the screenplays for the TV movies JUDGE DEE (1974) and THE NIGHT THAT PANICKED AMERICA (1975), as well as for the campy low budget film INVASION OF THE BEE GIRLS (1973).

Nicholas Meyer wasn't Paramount's first choice for the film. Meyer agreed to do STAR TREK II because he wanted to make a film called CONJURING. Parmount said that if STAR TREK II scored a hit film, then he could do whatever he wanted. Unfortunately, CONJURING was never made, and none of Nicholas Meyer's films since STAR TREK equaled TIME AFTER TIME.

STAR TREK: THE MOTION PICTURE had downplayed characterization. STAR TREK II fixed this when the director asked his actors to make script suggestions.

William Shatner explained how this worked in ENTERPRISE MAGAZINE #10. He said, "Under the best of circumstances, a drama is formed through the interaction of the writer, the director and the actors. That certainly took place here. The people coming in for the first time, even though both of

THE WRATH OF KHAN

them were Trek aficionados, were unacquainted with the details that we knew after so many years. So yes, we were consulted quite a bit."

ENTER SAAVIK

The primary cast was hired before Meyer, but he chose the supporting players. He wanted Kirstie Alley for Saavik. Meyer liked the way she moved. He felt that she was a perfect compliment for Nimoy, and Spock was her mentor.

Early scripts and the movie novelization reveal that Saavik is half-Vulcan and half-Romulan. Paramount ran an early coming attractions trailer for theater owners in the style of the old STAR TREK TV coming attractions trailers. In one scene Kirk and Spock discuss that Saavik is half-

Romulan. It was cut from the final print.

Meyer wanted romance in his film. He said, "The romance was very, very slight, and I liked it. I thought it was funny in the movie because here's Saavik, who is half-way in love with Admiral Kirk, and she knows that that's completely inappropriate. The moment she finds out that Admiral Kirk has a son—it just makes a heck of a lot of sense to her. What we did is we made a major change in the order of the plot, and she never learned that he was Kirk's son until near the end of the movie in the final version, so all that stuff didn't make any sense any more."

Kirstie Alley had a lot to learn. She made her movie debut in this feature. Alley has gone on to many things since, including a highly successful run as one of the ensemble of actors in the last several years of CHEERS.

Describing her work in STAR TREK II, Meyer said, "She had no experience whatsoever. She was getting advice from all sides, and the studio kept trying to make it more of a 'tits and ass' performance. I said, 'No, no, no. That's real. You're in the Navy. You're a pro. Just do your job. You're good; you're at the top of your class there.' My favorite thing about her was that you had the feeling of the staggering, competent Lt. Saavik, and that was important to me. That was what I wanted to get across. I think the performance is much more interesting for that reason."

THE SAAVIK QUESTION

Kirstie's agent requested a huge salary increase for STAR TREK III. Harve Bennett and Leonard Nimoy dropped her. Alley later expressed surprise, denying Bennett's public remarks that she demanded a huge fee and pointing out that Paramount never made a counter offer. This may have been intended as an object lesson to the supporting actors, demonstrating that the studio wouldn't buckle under demands.

Nicholas Meyer didn't like Robin Curtis as Saavik in STAR TREK III and IV. He wanted Kirstie Alley when he returned to direct STAR TREK VI: THE UNDISCOVERED COUNTRY. She wasn't available, so he replaced Saavik with a different character. Roddenberry once said Alley was too Beverly Hills for Saavik.

Ricardo Montalban returned as Khan. He hired a personal trainer to get fit and looked terrific by the time of the filming. Montalban liked the script and admired the directing of TIME AFTER TIME.

Meyer praised Montalban, saying, "He's living proof that good manners don't have to be bought. He is funny; he is very funny, a completely unjaded person. The question that everybody always asks me is, 'Is that his chest?' Unfortunately, yes."

THE RETURN OF KHAN

Montalban studied Khan in "Space Seed," and brought that bravura performance to his first day of filming. Meyer recalled, "When we first started working, we started with the scene in the cargo bay. It was six minutes of monologue with twenty-three camera moves back and forth. He knew the lines cold and I showed him the

moves and he got it perfectly the first time we walked through it.

"The performance was very different than what you see; it was on the ceiling. I thought omigod! I said, 'Now that we got the whole thing lined up perfectly, lets talk for a minute about interpretation. You know, I think you are much more powerful and much more dangerous if you're very quiet. If the audience doesn't know what you're capable of. Laurence Olivier once said, Never show an audience your top, because if you do, they'll know you have no place to go. It's better to keep it locked down. The thing about Olivier and Brando is that you can't relax watching them because you never know what the hell they're going to do.'

"I didn't even have to finish this sentence

because the man is really smart. He said, 'Oh yes, I see. Much better, ahhh.' (Nods head.) The whole performance came together from that single thing.

Meyer continued, "It just clicked with him, and he said, 'Oh, I know I need to be directed because I don't know, I can't be out there. I can't watch myself.' Actors almost never do that. I said, 'That is great! We're going to get along just fine.' He would not lift an eyebrow without saying, 'What do you think if I . . . ?' and I would say yes or no and so on."

FACING DEATH

Meyer revealed that the death of Spock affected the actors. "Everybody stood around on the stage in tears," he recalled, "which was very surprising to me because I'm not that experienced as a movie director and I was amazed at how moved they were. The next day at the dailies, the same thing. Everybody cried."

He continued, "After hearing, 'You can't go in there, you can't go. . . ' You gotta be wondering, 'What's happening to him?' You want to see what's going on there.

"It's a matter of choice; of taste. I would rather underplay and let the audience imagination rise to meet something halfway. From what I've seen of the series (Meyer was shown "Space Seed," "Charlie X" and "Let That Be Your Last Battlefield" as sample episodes), I think they overacted or showed too much.

"My attitude has changed perceptively. I don't know whether it was the actors themselves or the characters,

THE WRATH OF KHAN

but when I was watching this death scene and I realized that *I* was choked up, I thought, well, we have now transcended the subject matter. This is no longer simply about a man with pointy ears, which is how I'd felt because I didn't know it that well."

Nicholas Meyer wanted to call the film STAR TREK II: THE UNDISCOVERED COUNTRY— referring to death and the future. Paramount balked. Meyer never liked the final title choice. He eventually used his title when he directed STAR TREK VI.

SPECIAL CONNECTION

Producer Robert Sallin hired Jim Danforth as a special effects consultant for THE WRATH OF KHAN, the role Douglas Trumbull played for the first film.

Danforth created a budget and a schedule for the producer to use when comparing bids from subcontractors. Sallin met with a number of firms but finally gave Industrial Light & Magic (ILM) the entire film due to the short schedule.

ILM opened in June of 1975 when John Dykstra assembled a team of talented craftsmen for George Lucas and Gary Kurtz. After STAR WARS was released, ILM became a household word and Dykstra won an Oscar.

Paramount wanted good relations with George Lucas, so they hired Industrial Light and Magic, bypassing Douglas Trumbull and John Dykstra. There may have been lingering concerns that Trumbull and Dykstra contributed to the cost overruns on

STAR TREK: THE MOTION PICTURE.

Douglas Trumbull claimed he had underbid ILM by $1.5 million. Trumbull's ire increased when he saw that STAR TREK II: THE WRATH OF KHAN reused special effects from STAR TREK: THE MOTION PIC- TURE not credited on screen. Neither Trumbull nor Dykstra have worked on STAR TREK films since.

When ILM filmed the heavy Enterprise model built by Trumbull, they offered to pay a consult- ing fee if his people advised them how to work with the cumber- some prop. Trumbull turned them down flat.

INDUSTRIAL LIGHT & MAGIC

ILM stores every- thing a special effects unit might need on their premises. It includes a model shop, a carpentry shop, a machine shop, an electronics shop, a roto- scope department, an optical printing depart- ment and a film control department that coordi- nates film elements for special effects.

John Dykstra devel- oped the motion control camera for ILM. It could be programmed to repeat the same maneu- ver over and over again and revolve on seven dif- ferent axis of movement. The camera was original- ly called the "Dykstraflex." After Dykstra split with ILM to form Apogee, ILM renamed the camera as the "Flex." It has since been modified many times.

While Nicholas Meyer filmed his actors, ILM worked on the special effects. The accelerated production schedule did not allow them to wait until the live action shooting finished.

STAR TREK: THE MOTION PICTURE required five hundred special effects shots; THE WRATH OF KHAN used one hundred fifty. The difference isn't too visible on screen because THE WRATH OF KHAN makes better use of its effects. Most appear in the space battles between the Enterprise and the Defiant.

STAR TREK is known for interesting spacecraft designs. The Enterprise broke films away from using traditional cigar-shaped rockets. The new STAR TREK II spacecraft, the Reliant, recombined the best elements of the Enterprise in an unusual fashion.

THE RELIANT

The Reliant was designed at Paramount and constructed at Industrial Light & Magic under the guidance of supervising model maker Steve Gawley. ILM had inherited Douglas Trumbull's cumbersome model of the Enterprise. They wanted a Reliant that wouldn't require half a dozen people to move for photography.

They shaped the hull of the Reliant from vacuformed plastic. The completed model was so light it could be handled by two people. Gawley's crew included Sean Casey, Mike Fulmer, Brian Chin, Steve Sanders, Martin Brenneis, Jeff Mann, Bill George, Bob Diepenbrock and Larry Tan.

They constructed arger sections for close-ups, especially when the overhead portion of the Reliant is shattered by a phaser blast. Explosive charges inside the section blew out pre-packed pieces of plastic scrap, giving the illusion of an exploding ship. Jettisoning the interior pieces made the damage look greater than it was. They formed the exploded model from wax easily remolded for additional shots. The addition of opticals of the phaser beam and the explosion element enhanced the effect.

Sets from STAR TREK: THE MOTION PICTURE were reused to save money. The Regula One spacelab raided by Khan was the orbiting office complex from ST:TMP. Only diehard fans noticed.

COMPUTER CRAFT

Computer graphics are now common in motion pictures. STAR TREK II used experimental computer animation for the Genesis Device.

Since the image on screen appears on the Enterprise computer, it was intended to look animated rather than realistic.

The sequence occupies sixty seconds of screen time but conveys information vital to the story. It took ten artists five months to complete it. Jim Viellieux and his ILM crew developed a new computer painting program. In the next decade, ILM advanced this process to produce live action sequences indistinguishable from reality.

ILM created all the special effects. They occasionally farmed out some shots due to time constraints. Former Industrial Light and Magic technician Peter Kuran had left to open his own small facility in Hollywood near Santa Monica Boulevard. He did subcontract work for ILM. His outfit, Visual Concepts Engineering, made some of the phaser effects, including when Kirk's hand phaser vaporized the Ceti Eel that crawled out of Chekov's head.

The transporter effect was different from that seen in STAR TREK: THE MOTION PICTURE. Paramount supervised Visual Concepts Engineering to produce the effect. After several false starts, they settled on merging two pillars of light. Peter Kuran originally wanted to materialize people in layers, beginning with the skeleton, then the circulatory system, and finally the rest of the body. His inspiration came from the 1960s OUTER LIMITS episode "The Special One." Bob Sallin preferred a more conventional approach.

THE CLIMACTIC BATTLE

The climactic space battle inside the Mutara Nebula was the most spectacular moment of the film. In a nod to classic submarine war pictures, the two vessels hunt each other without the benefit of sensors like oldtime submarines, each waiting for the other to make a mistake. The sequence is also reminiscent of the original STAR TREK episode "Balance of Terror."

ILM filmed the space battle in a large structure near San Francisco called the Cow Palace. The purple nebula effect uses a "cloud tank," a huge glass tank filled part way with fresh water topped slowly with salt water. The lighter salt water floats along the top, but the area where the salt water and fresh water merge forms an inversion layer. Slowly injecting a solution of white rubber latex with turkey basters creates clouds in the water. The resulting white cloud is tinted with colored lights giving the shades of the nebula.

Photographing the cloud at the rate of one frame per second, rather than the standard 24, allows unusual lighting effects. Special effects co-supervisor Ken Ralston accomplished this by walking around the tank shining a light into it at key points. It looks like ball lightning or strange discharge inside the nebula.

WORKING ON THE ENTERPRISE

ILM altered the Enterprise model they inherited from the first film to better suit their needs. The surface was repainted with a non-gloss white to prevent reflected light when photographed. Otherwise the glare picked up the blue screen, resulting in optical holes.

Some people from the special effects crew of STAR TREK: THE MOTION PICTURE returned for STAR TREK II. Returning Art Director Mike Minor compared the two experiences.

"I thought the first movie was pretty washed out, visually," he candidly admitted in a 1982 STARLOG interview. "It had no heart. Part of that can be traced back to the design element. During the first picture, all the sets were buttoned up. In other words, the bridge was built as one, solid structure. It could never be opened up to get a camera into it for a better angle. That camera was going to be inside a real ship and we were going to wander around the vessel with it in a very slow, stately manner. That situation forced the filmmakers into a corner. They had to use very dim lighting on the sets. They couldn't let the proper amount of lights onto them because everything was so cramped."

Some people at ILM disliked the design of the Enterprise, and were secretly happy when they blew it up. Production Designer Joe Jennings recognized that the look of the Enterprise was an integral part of STAR TREK. Jennings told CINEFANTASTIQUE, "It's part of the STAR TREK universe now. The fans are familiar with how the Enterprise looks, so it all has a sort of de facto existence, a bogus logic. You have to work with

that, and I think a production designer has to realize it. Directors, too. Sometimes they're hard to convince and you have to do a sales job. You have to say, 'Look, that won't work, that place isn't there. You can't get there from here and the fans know it. If you want to do your own outer space movie then go off and do it, but don't call it STAR TREK."

Mike Minor drew the storyboards ILM followed for the special effects. One shot occured during the first encounter between the Reliant and the Enterprise. Kirk saved the day after the Reliant surprised them. The Reliant fled in a tight shot, then suddenly emerged from behind the Enterprise and escaped over the top of it. The two ships appeared about to collide.

Another impressive contribution was what Mike called the "can-opener" shot. This occured when the Reliant fired on the Enterprise and the beam traced along the hull, slicing it open. They used a large section of the Enterprise hull in this close-up. It was made out of wax and softened under the hot studio lights.

They sculpted a hole in the hull a little bit at a time, photographing it several frames at a time, creating an illusion of a swatch being cut. As this happened, they cut away to a live action shot of panic inside the ship. Originally shots were planned showing crewmen yanked out into space through the gash in the hull. Time considerations cut it from the schedule.

A TIGHT SCHEDULE

Shooting for STAR TREK II began November 9, 1981, and ended on January 29, 1982. Nicholas Meyer immediately finished the editing process he had begun during filming. Ordinarily editing begins after principal photography ends, but at the end of the shooting day, Meyer went to the editing room. He arrived at the studio before sunrise to prep shots and left the editing room after nightfall.

Mike Minor budgeted $980,000 for set construction. Paramount insisted the figure be cut by $300,000. It threw a monkey wrench into many plans.

"We were planning, for instance, to build a real Eden cave with a huge waterfall sixty feet high," Mike revealed. "It was going to fill up Stage 15 at

THE WRATH OF KHAN

Paramount, which has a huge tank in it. We were planning to build all of the cliff faces, and we couldn't do it. So we cut back from the scale of things to doing the bubble effect in a fifty by fifty area and the rest accomplished through a fairly successful matte painting done by ILM."

Matte painters Frank Ordaz and Chris Evans labored to create a glittering illusion, the Genesis, or Eden, Cave with its massive underground waterfall flowing into a beautiful lake. They painted the matte on glass, enabling the filmmakers to achieve the illusion of movement in the "water." A rotating wheel with cotton moved behind cut-out shapes of the channels of water.

THE FUTURE

The tight budget and limited time cut into other plans, requiring careful rethinking and imaginative shortcuts. One change involved abandoning an elaborate set of Kirk's condo in San Francisco.

"We wanted to see him coming up the stairs from the bottom level," Mike explained, "but it just wasn't possible. We had to build it on one level and cut $40 thousand out of that set. With one thing and another, I felt happy that I could at least get two miniature buildings thrown out against the backdrop. They're just a throwaway, but the elevator is going up and down past him in that opening sequence in the apartment at night. There's something going on in the middleground so you believe what's outside the window a bit more, hopefully."

Miniature buildings in front of a painted cyclorama of the distant landscape portrayed futuristic San Francisco at night. Lighted elevators moving up the side of the miniature add a special touch.

They cut another corner by borrowing the painting from 20th Century Fox. It had appeared a decade earlier in THE TOWERING INFERNO.

BUILDING A PLANET

STAR TREK: THE MOTION PICTURE used location work that wasn't in the budget for STAR TREK II. Instead they used a sound stage, just as they had for the old TV episodes.

They constructed sets on Paramount's stage 8, using wooden frames for sand dunes. The mounds were camouflaged with sand and

Fuller's earth, a type of artificial dirt. Fuller's earth was blown around by four huge Ritter fans resembling caged airplane propellers. It made a sand storm.

A sixty foot long sand dune stood in the background, continuing offstage after dropping at a 45 degree angle. The planetary exteriors were draped with a gigantic painted cyclorama, a painting on canvas, to represent the sky.

Building it was only half the problem. The blowing sand and Fuller's earth made shooting hazardous. Everyone wore eye goggles and breathing filters to prevent the fine swirling particles from getting into their lungs. The cameras and sound equipment were covered in plastic shrouds to prevent clogging the delicate mechanisms.

THE WRATH OF KHAN

The script originally called for an ice planet, but they thought sand dunes would be more interesting. Three days of slogging around in blowing dirt showed them the error of their ways. Walter Koenig and Paul Winfield walked in space suits that only contained five minutes of air.

Then there was the Ceti Eel. The thing had the nasty habit of burrowing into a person's head through their ear and eating their brain. An early draft of the screenplay called for a simplified version of the creature that attached itself to the base of the skull. Bob Sallin didn't like it, but didn't know what else to do. Then he saw a slug one morning, and the idea grew from there.

The adult eel is only seen once, early in the film. Khan showed it before picking up a baby with a set of prongs. The adult was a simple puppet with rods attached beneath the tail and a mechanism for operating the jaws. The baby eels were cut out of foam rubber, covered with slime and pulled along on a nearly invisible monofilament line.

They modeled three versions of Chekov's ear in sections. The first was shot dry, with no blood. The second was filmed with just a little blood trickling out of the ear. The third, very bloody shot is called the "Fangoria shot," after the gory horror magazine.

HEDGING THEIR BETS

Nicholas Meyer planned to kill Spock as the script demanded. Paramount backed away from the idea and, over the director's objections and without his participation, filmed additional scenes in April 1982, two months before release.

Producer Robert Sallin directed a crew from Industrial Light & Magic at Golden Gate Park in San Francisco. They shot the footage now seen at the end of the film when Spock's coffin sits in the jungle representing the Genesis planet.

Originally the film ended with the funeral scene. The new footage shows an intact coffin at rest on the planet's surface, leaving an unanswered question in the mind of the viewer.

Nicholas Meyer objected, but Paramount, and not the director, had the right of final cut. Harve Bennett conceived the final scene. He wouldn't bend to Meyer's complaints. The director believed the film lied to the audience. It left the ending wide open. Just as the studio wanted, it ended on a note of hope rather than finality.

Harve Bennett explained their decision. It was partially a response to the angry mail. Bennett said, "Leonard was getting threatening letters. This was a serious thing and I felt that the compromise we had to make, with Nick's blessing (reluctant though that was) was that we made an ambiguity out of the ending by saying 'There are always possibilities.' We said, 'Who knows with Vulcans?'

"I have said once or twice at STAR TREK gatherings that I have always tried to be fair. I have a great affection for these people even when they're so proprietary that they come over and tell you that you can't do it your way, you have to do it my way. These people keep that franchise. It is a business. They keep it healthy and strong. They are its lifeblood. So you do not disregard that. To be fair you've got to give clues and those were the clues we dropped.

"We also shot an insert of Leonard putting his hand on McCoy and saying, 'remember.' The very close shot of that wasn't Leonard's hand."

They redid that shot in STAR TREK III: THE SEARCH FOR SPOCK because Nimoy insisted that his own hand be used.

Bennett continued, "Then I sent a crew to Golden Gate Park, which is Genesis, in San Francisco and we shot the casket. By so doing we said, unbeknownst to them it has soft-landed. I think that was the right series of compromises.

We said Spock dies. We do not wish to compromise the impact of that, but this is science fiction and there are always possibilities."

BACK-PEDALING

Meyer said the studio and Nimoy were having second thoughts. He explained, "There was a flurry of back-pedaling about this and that, and you're going to kill the series. My interest was not in the series. My interest was in this movie."

The director felt the actors were thinking of the film too much like a TV episode where the end of the hour brings everything back to the status quo and life goes on unchanged.

"The sensibility that I was trying to bring to it was completely separate," Meyer explained. "I said, 'Big things are going to happen here, and everything is not going to be the same at the end as it was in the beginning.' It's got everybody aging. That's antithetical to the notion of coming back to where you were. Aging and death. Kirk wears glasses. That was a kind of a shock (to them) at the beginning, but when they got to know me and trust me, then instead of being a liability, it became a challenge. Everybody got real excited. I think they breathed new life into those roles, they got so worked up about it. I loved them. I like the actors. I had a great time. It was fun to shoot with them."

Despite Meyer opposing the studio over the end of the film, he came back to help with STAR TREK IV and to direct STAR TREK VI.

Paramount ultimately chose not to kill a popular element of STAR TREK. It's not surprising. STAR TREK II grossed a healthy $80 million, and came in under budget and on time. The series was successfully relaunched. Soon STAR TREK III would go into production.

THE WRATH OF KHAN

STAR TREK 3

THE SEARCH FOR SPOCK

THE REVIEW

After THE WRATH OF KHAN, fans demanded Spock back. Paramount answered their pleas two years later, sending the STAR TREK crew on THE SEARCH FOR SPOCK. They returned to the Genesis planet.

The Klingon villains looked and acted the same as in every appearance in the original 1960s series. They lacked subtlety. Black-hearted Commander Kruge killed anyone to get the secret of Genesis. He met a fitting end on the Genesis planet.

Kirk's son David died. Harve Bennett claimed David had to die because he "cheated" in developing the Genesis Device.

Industrial Light & Magic blew up the Enterprise as Kirk and his crew watched from the surface of Genesis. The vision of the remains of the Enterprise as a falling star was quite effective.

Vulcan resurrection savedSpock at the end. It was no weirder than pon farr.

It was good to get Spock back.

Spock died in the second feature film, or did he? The Enterprise is put at risk to learn his fate.

STAR TREK III: THE SEARCH FOR SPOCK

STAR TREK II: THE WRATH OF KHAN scored big at the box office in the summer of 1982, grossing $80 million. Discussions immediately began for a sequel.

The filmmakers recalled Spock's intact coffin on the Genesis planet at the end of STAR TREK II. This offered their hope for a sequel. Harve Bennett picked up on the scene when Spock mind-melded with McCoy and said, "Remember." Without a sequel, this would have been Spock's good-bye to his old friend. Bennett used the scene to launch his story treatment.

THE FANS OBJECT

An early story outline omitted the mind-meld scene. The outline circulated in fandom. Some people, including Bjo Trimble, dismissed it as the work of "a talented fan." When Majel Barrett publicly declared it the genuine article,

Bjo angrily accused her of lying. She claimed Barrett was "just trying to be mischievous."

Susan Sackett, of Gene Roddenberry's staff, refused to confirm or deny the authenticity of the document. Everyone maintained a stony silence, adding credence to the authenticity.

Bennett finally admitted the outline was real after STAR TREK III: THE SEARCH FOR SPOCK appeared.

One controversy remained unchanged in the final film: they blew up the Enterprise. Gene Roddenberry adamantly opposed it just as he had Spock's death, but Roddenberry was just a consultant with no power

EARLY STORY IDEAS

Bennett began with a poem in a STAR TREK fan magazine. In it Kirk felt impelled to return to the world holding his old friend's remains.

The earliest plans for the storyline cast the Romulans as the villains rather than the Klingons. Nimoy suggested the Klingons, even though the Romulans of original STAR TREK were more interesting.

This story idea had people on the Enterprise see visions of Spock. In the final film, only McCoy had visions. McCoy blamed himself for Spock's death, and took a leave of absence on Vulcan to clear his mind. Later versions of the script dropped this part of the story.

The Enterprise returned to the Genesis planet after Sarek expressed anger that his son's body wasn't returned to him. He believed Vulcan science might have saved him. Kirk agreed to return Spock's body, forcing them to retrieve it.

IMAGES OF SPOCK

The outline revealed that Spock left information in McCoy's mind, but didn't indicate its importance. An early scene, later changed, showed the Romulans destroying an orbiting Federation ship. In the film, the Klingons destroy the vessel that brought David and Saavik to the Genesis planet. The outline has the Romulans find dilithium crystals on the Genesis planet.

Klingons appear in the outline when they protest the Genesis device to the Federation. This finally appeared STAR TREK IV. The outline omits the sequence when the Klingons buy information about the Genesis device and then eliminate their source. This Klingon subplot remained undeveloped.

As Kirk requested permission from Starfleet to return to the Genesis planet, he saw visions of Spock. Instead Starfleet put Kirk under house arrest, and reassigned the core crew of the Enterprise. Sulu rescued him, inspiring the filmed sequence when the crew stole the Enterprise and rescued McCoy from confinement.

ROMULAN CONNECTION

The remainder of the story is different. A long-haired, bearded Spock lurked on the surface of the Genesis planet killing Romulans at night in their mining encampment. Spock had amnesia. The Enterprise crew took Spock and the Romulan ship and escaped before Genesis imploded into a black hole.

They surrendered to a Federation ship. Spock regained his memory, and all ended well.

This plot led to a script.

Paramount asked Nimoy to play Spock again. Money was no longer an issue. He'd been well paid for the first two STAR TREK films. This time he wanted something else.

Nimoy casually mentioned that he wanted to direct. Paramount head honcho Michael Eisner liked the idea. By April 1983 everyone was convinced. Nimoy reported to the lot to prepare the movie for production. Producer Harve Bennett regularly met with Nimoy to discuss script develop-

ment, even before paper was signed.

THE NEXT STEP

Nimoy took it in stride. He never thought his fellow cast members might fear his directing. They thought Nimoy might make a Spock picture, virtually excluding their own characters. Shatner was very worried.

Nimoy recalled, "I must be really naive about this, I really must. I was surprised that there was so much interest and concern about that. The interests and concerns are valid. I just didn't perceive the potential problems or friction that other people perceive. My fellow actors were concerned about it before we started doing the picture. I simply took it as fact that I had their best interests at heart, that I would know their characters well. I certainly knew their potential well and would try to explore it.

"That was one of the things I argued in that period of time when I was asking for the job. I said, I know these people. I know these characters. I know what can be done with them. So it was ironic for me and kind of startling that the very thing I thought would have the greatest success with was the cast, and that was the major question that people were more concerned about.

"I didn't have anybody say, 'What do you know about shooting a $16 million movie with spaceships and planets exploding, fire scenes and fights and people falling off cliffs and stuff like that?' Nobody asked me about that. They said, 'What about the actors?'"

Nimoy discovered a sense of competition between the actors he hadn't previously noticed.

"That's a strange thing to say," he admitted. "I'm an actor, have been in television and films since 1950. This was the first time that I had it really enunciated to me that some of the actors in the cast were concerned (about) my competitiveness. I think we got over that very quickly. They saw that I was well prepared, that I was well intended where they were concerned, and that they were given the opportunity to develop and have some fun in their performances."

DIRECTING DEBUT

STAR TREK III: THE SEARCH FOR SPOCK was Nimoy's feature film debut. His previous directing experience had been on episodic television for THE POWERS OF MATTHEW STAR, NIGHT GALLERY and T.J. HOOKER. He later went on to direct STAR TREK IV, THREE MEN AND A BABY, THE GOOD MOTHER, FUNNY ABOUT LOVE and HOLY MATRIMONY. Only the two STAR TREK movies and THREE MEN AND A BABY were box office successes.

Shooting on STAR TREK III began on August 15, 1983. They planned 49 days of principal photography. Nimoy also acted in the film. It didn't create problems because he didn't appear until late in the picture. STAR TREK III completed principal photography October 21, 1983.

Nimoy described his approach to directing at a press conference, saying, "I'm probably somewhere in between Bob Wise and Nicholas Meyer. Not as precise as Bob, not as imaginative or rough-edged as Nick. I think the major difference, and for me the most important difference, is my attitude toward the story and the actors. They (Wise and Meyer) are looking for a different kind of final product than I am."

AN UNFORTUNATE ABSENCE

Nimoy and Bennett discovered that Shatner wanted to be in every scene. After many complaints, Bennett told Shatner, "'Bill, I'll tell you what you are. You are a quarterback who wants to call the play, run back, throw the pass, catch the pass, score the touchdown and lead the cheers.' He hugged me and said, 'You're right. I can't help it.'"

Bennett chose not to use the Carol Marcus character. He wanted to kill David because he cheated using protomatter in the Genesis device, making the planet was unstable. "I confess to being old-fashioned," Bennett stated. "There is in my vision such a thing as ultimate retribution. The reason David dies, structurally, is because he's messed with mother nature. He allowed himself to bend the rules at the wrong time, in the wrong place. He's there on that planet for only that reason. The whole story dates back to David putting protomatter in the matrix. The death of Spock, everything rests on his shoulders if you want to blame him for it."

This created two problems. Pseudo-science should have a logical basis, and the Genesis planet made no sense! The explosion of a terraforming device couldn't create a planet out of nothing. It only changes existing planets.

Carol Marcus was dropped rather than confront whether she knew David cheated. When David was killed, she was nowhere around. Vonda McIntyre's novelization fills in that gap for fans. The real reason for the omission was budget.

TRADE OFFS

Another glaring absence is Amanda at Spock's resurrection. Bennett explained her absence, saying, "All she would have contributed was sympathy. The economy of the story was that Kirk and crew get Spock back. Family is secondary. That would have depreciated the moment when Spock says, 'Your name is Jim.' Then we'd have to cut to mother and she would say, 'Oh my god, he speaks!'"

Bennett dealt with trade-offs. Kirk found Spock but lost the Enterprise. He described this as "balance." Gene Roddenberry and the fans objected, and regarded it as a gimmick.

"The death of the Enterprise caused serious ripples," Bennett admitted. He found it strange that no one minded David Marcus' death. "That's ass-backwards for me. (Destroying) the Enterprise is a burden I take full responsibility for. I will justify it to the end and once again I think I have been playing fair. My choice was a humanistic choice. It began as a writer's problem. Usually it happens when you reach a sticky point. I had a whole justification for it.

"Oliver Hazard Perry of the U.S. Navy scuttled the Niagara at the battle of Lake Erie and won the battle as a result. He was rowed on a rowboat to another ship and took command. Perry happens to be one of James T. Kirk's great heroes. There is a model of the Niagara in Kirk's quarters for those who love STAR TREK trivia. The scuttling of the ship to achieve the greater good is a tactic. Also, with the death his son, and the hopelessness of the situation, it seemed like the right solution."

THE CAPER

Nimoy supervised the first rough cut after completing principal photography. Special effects editors Bil Kimberlin and Jay Ignaszewski provided him with black and white work prints of the visual effects. The effects shots were still being refined but were complete enough to be viewed. This was better than seeing a black piece of film reading "scene missing."

Nimoy decided the structure didn't work. The caper sequence with Kirk, Sulu, Scotty, Uhura and Chekov freeing Dr. McCoy and stealing the Enterprise was scattered among other plot elements. It fractured the light touch of the conspiracy amid the harder edged scenes of the Klingons in space and on the Genesis planet. Nimoy assembled the caper into a long sequence to create cohesion.

The director revealed that the pon farr sequence was Roddenberry's idea. Saavik's solution to Spock's problem isn't specified in the film. Fans who understand pon farr know what happened between the frames. The studio feared the sequence would draw laughs and wanted it cut, but relented when preview audiences failed to laugh.

Very little of the interior of a Klingon ship had been shown before. Many things had to be designed. Paramount production artist Tom Lay designed some of the interior details. One was the medical examination table in the sick bay of Commander Kruge's Bird of Prey. It resembled the outline of a serpent with a head coiled over the head of the patient, a decidedly dramatic image. The instrument panel over the diagnostic bed was blood red and shaped like a serpent's mouth. The side of the bed was fully equipped with fangs!

A HAPPY ASSOCIATION

The happy association between Paramount and Industrial Light & Magic continued with STAR TREK III. The schedule wasn't quite as breathless as that for THE WRATH OF KHAN. Industrial Light & Magic became more directly involved with the film earlier in the production. Special effects supervisor Ken Ralston created the storyboards with Nilo Rodis and David Carson. They planned a unified approach with a consistent style.

ILM technicians Warren Franklin, Nilo Rodis and David Carson prepared the storyboards in November of 1982 after Harve Bennett provided them with the original two page outline.

They brainstormed ideas for special effects sequences.

The trio worked with Nimoy and Bennett, as well as Tom Lay, a production artist at Paramount. They storyboarded the entire script, consulting scene by scene on the most interesting approaches. The storyboards included initial ideas for the look of the main sets and initial designs for the Excelsior, the Klingon Bird of Prey and the space dock.

ILM model makers Bill George and Michael Fulmer used the storyboard sketches to prepare rough prototype designs later further refined in the model-making workshops. The special effects team always planned ahead, avoiding the surprises encountered on THE WRATH OF KHAN.

Early prototypes previewed finished models. Bill George altered a prototype of a space station design for everyone to see the final product before making changes. It was like sketching in 3-D.

ILM created more than 120 special effects shots. Director Leonard Nimoy spoke of the amazing studio, saying, "I found the people at Industrial Light and Magic totally supportive and wildly imaginative. They are film lovers. They want to be turned on, just like the actors. They have a high-tech background, but they never employed their knowledge to coerce or manipulate me."

SECURITY CONCERNS

Paramount wanted secrecy. ILM only got the parts of the script they needed, but there was no way to keep a lid on the destruction of the Enterprise since ILM handled the whole job. Word leaked out more than six months before the film's release. Gene Roddenberry opposed the idea. It didn't arouse a furor, and the planned destruction remained unchanged.

The studio wanted no more leaks. ILM also had security concerns due to other projects. When John Chilberg, the art director for STAR TREK III, visited ILM, he was led into a private room where STAR TREK storyboards were kept separate from those of other films. They instructed him not to look at storyboards hanging on a wall on the opposite side of the room. They were from the George Lucas and Steven Spielberg coproduction INDIANA JONES

AND THE TEMPLE OF DOOM.

ILM maintained an enviable security record while Paramount suffered years of losses. A ring of thieves climbed the back fence and stole costumes from the Paramount lot in the late 1980s. The ringleader was finally caught with more than one hundred STAR TREK costumes in his possession. Other thieves backed a van up to a chain link fence, cut through and loaded dozens of costumes until fleeing a security guard.

SPACE JUNK

STAR TREK III saved money by reusing props, sets and costumes from STAR TREK II.

Robert Fletcher refurbished the costumes, and designed new ones when needed. Sarek wore a new costume when he visited Kirk early in the film. Fletcher's design consisted of a stone-studded breastplate based on two thousand year old Jewish clothing.

Designs for the new Klingon costumes were borrowed from feudal Japan. Previous Klingon costumes seen in STAR TREK: THE MOTION PICTURE were badly damaged during an episode of MORK AND MINDY. They were part of a pile of "space junk" for the last season of that TV series.

McCoy entered a specially designed bar on the space station. A video game featured a holographic tabletop display of World War One biplanes in mock conflict. Cameron Birnie redressed the Enterprise sick bay for the bar.

Other refurbished sets also appeared. Production designer John

Chilberg repainted the black floor of the bridge a dark gray for enhanced lighting purposes.

Associate producer Ralph Winter served as Nimoy's liaison with ILM. He kept each side aware of what the other was doing. Nimoy said ILM welcomed ideas and liked being included in the early development of a film.

THE SPACE DOCK

The space dock figures prominently in the early part of the film. Much hard work went into the model during the first several weeks of production. Special effects photographer Scott Farrar and others generated footage of the space dock interior. Smoke was used on the set to enhance the illusion of depth. They had to experiment to make the interior appear vast enough to house gigantic starships.

The smoke caused background images to appear slightly hazy, as though seen from a distance. They put blue gels over the lights while shooting in smoke. Farrar and his team used a diffusion filter on the camera rather than smoke to achieve greater control for filming the light passes. The models of the Enterprise and the Excelsior weren't photographed inside the space dock model. No ship models were built at this scale.

The Enterprise's departure from space dock was the first spacecraft shot filmed by ILM for THE SEARCH FOR SPOCK. Filming inside the space dock was difficult because the ships couldn't appear to move even though the camera was moving.

THE SEARCH FOR SPOCK

They shot test footage in black and white to learn to match the ship models to the space dock interior. They plotted each shot on a grid system on the Movieola editing machine to prevent movement. The space dock sequences took more than two months to complete. Farrar and his team filmed the background. Then Don Dow added the spaceships to the footage.

GARAGE IN SPACE

The logic of an enclosed space dock in outer space is not explained. It looks dramatic but isn't practical. Such a huge structure certainly wouldn't require a "garage door" such as the one the Enterprise escaped through in a dramatic but illogical scene.

Lights on the space dock made it hard to shoot. It couldn't be too bright or they'd create a lens flare. The lighted door panels had to be shot on a separate pass of the camera. Lights had to be mounted on the door to shine into special boxes to create an even lighting level.

A striking image appeared when the Enterprise was viewed through a window from inside a restaurant. Nimoy went to the Industrial Light and Magic facility in Marin County for this shot. It was the only live action footage not shot at Paramount Studios. The simple set needed forty extras, including Grace Lee Whitney. The greater portion of it appeared as a matte painting. The window displaying the Enterprise was a large ILM blue screen.

SPACE CREATURES

ILM worked with Paramount photographic director Charlie Correll on the studio lot to create the creature scenes. One sequence involved the reptile dog kept on the bridge of the Klingon ship by Commander Kruge. Similar creatures have not been seen on STAR TREK since.

The pet was created by Ken Ralston's crew at ILM, including David Sosalla, Kirk Thatcher and John Reed. Sosalla also worked with Chris Walas on the movie GREMLINS, released at the same time as THE SEARCH FOR SPOCK.

The creature employed no optical effects or animation. The body was operated from off stage. Cables and mechanical hand controls operated air bladders beneath the creature's skin and articulated skull. The skull acted like a hand puppet for closeups. Ken Ralston remained outside the view of the camera as he reached into the lizard-dog through one side of the body. Ralston's thumb operated a sensitive spring mechanism producing precise movements of the creature's jaw.

The fur looked strange. It was pieces of cheap wigs reassembled to give a mangy appearance. Different color wigs contributed to the effect. The creature's coat was then soaked with water to complete the look.

The lizard-dog never left its spot. Careful movements by the off-camera creature operators made it seem ready to get up from its comfortable position at its master's feet at any given moment. Ultimately the lizard-dog perished. A "dead" version of the creature was designed, but replaced by the articulated "live" version at the last moment.

Other creatures filmed on the Paramount lot included the worms Commander Kruge found when he opened Spock's coffin. The worms were moved by fishing lines strung around the set. Rods poked the worms, creating an illusion of motion. The larger worms were pulled with invisible fishing line wrapped around Kruge's arm.

FIRE IN THE SKY

The destruction of the Enterprise was planned as the biggest special effects scene. Many ILM technicians were STAR TREK fans. They were ambivalent about destroying the leg-

endary starship. They didn't destroy one of the original, expensive models but a breakaway model with special sections for close-ups of the demolition.

The Enterprise died in a series of shots. First the bridge section exploded as the vessel dove, displaying the familiar identification number. Then the saucer section was eaten away in a ripple of energy before also blowing up. Finally, in an infamous shot, the decimated starship fell towards the planet below. The camera cut away to Kirk and the others on the surface as they watched their ship plummet like a comet. Matte painter Coroleen Green created this effect.

A six foot saucer section was constructed of light weight styrene plastic for close-ups. It was photographed at four frames per second as acetone and other solvents dropped onto the surface making it appear to melt from intense heat. The technicians wore eye goggles as they sprayed the solvents from squeeze bottles. They covered their faces to avoid inhaling the fumes.

Initial test shots were unsuccessful. The chemicals remained visible, causing it to look as if the surface was pelted with acid rain. They finally found a spraying technique that worked.

They created fire effects by applying steel wool to key spots. The lighted steel wool created a burning glow, simulating burning in outer space. Burning oil melted the steel wool. When pieces of melting steel wool flew off, the fireworks were optically removed from completed footage.

FIRE ON THE BRIDGE

Full size sets were built for the interior of the Enterprise. Bob Dawson, the special effects supervisor for Paramount, took charge of these effects. Fiberglas turbolift doors made them more difficult. The material cannot safely burn with anyone around, so Dawson rebuilt the doors out of balsa wood. Nine inch steel tubes put behind the wooden doors contained small explosives packed with an agent treated with gasoline.

The full size sets could only be blown up once. It had to be done right the first time. The pipes behind the doors served as mortars, propelling the explosives to full effect. These, and other charges detonated by Dawson's pyrotechnics crew, brought a spectacular end to the Enterprise bridge set.

Dawson underestimated the impact of the explosions. One sent a powerful fireball down the supposedly safe corridor towards him. He couldn't escape, and spent several days in the hospital recoving from minor burns to his face and arms.

BUILDING GENESIS

A guide had to be constructed before the full scale Genesis planet sets could be built. This guide consisted of an eight foot by eight foot miniature cut into quarters for various crews on the Paramount lot. The miniature was based on production sketches. A three dimensional version acted as a guide for the studio carpenters.

This miniature included the mechanisms for the full size set to simulate earthquakes and ground cracking open. It required complicated workmanship. The final set was twenty-five feet in height.

They filmed the live action footage of the Genesis planet at Paramount. The destruction of the planet as seen on the surface was filmed on stage 15, the sound stage also known as the (Cecil B.) DeMille stage, after the famous director of THE TEN COMMANDMENTS and THE GREATEST SHOW ON EARTH. It is one of the largest sound stages in Hollywood. It had to be. The completed set for the Genesis planet was one hundred feet by three hundred feet.

The planetary setting contained a variety of sets representing the planet's surface as it underwent climatic and geologic changes. It included a desert, a jungle, an icy wasteland and the volcanic landscape where Commander Kruge and Captain Kirk fought their final battle as earthquakes decimated the planet.

Robert Dawson supervised the special effects created on the sound stage for the Genesis planet. They used plastic snow to create an illusion of snowfall for the winter scenes. Ritter fans supplied the winds for a blizzard. It proved so noisy when the fans blew at full blast that hand signals were needed to communicate.

IN-DOOR EARTHQUAKES

A fourteen man crew under Robert Dawson managed the live action destruction sequences filmed on stage fifteen. Dawson had created indoor earthquakes before for the television miniseries SHOGUN. Those earthquakes weren't as complex, but the basic techniques were the same.

Dawson needed several fissures to open up in the set. The fissures ran between twenty and sixty feet in length, averaging four or five feet across, and ten to twelve feet deep. They built the set on a raised truss system with a framework of four-by-four wooden beams in rows divided at six-foot intervals. Dawson and his construction team filled the spaces with slightly inclined sheets of lumber.

The wooden cross beams supporting the set were partially sawed through in the middle. A hinge and cables were attached to the weakened sections. Then the entire area was covered with sawdust and dirt and the final set constructed on top of it. They layered gray slag from an old steel mine as basic soil over a plywood base. It was finally peppered with decomposed granite, and covered with topsoil and various trees and other plants.

The cables pulled the wooden supports away as dirt and sawdust fell to create realistic looking fissures in the ground. William Shatner and other actors worked with the effects live on the set, complete with a pyrotechnic light show.

THE END OF GENESIS

Other sections of the Genesis stage showed more ravaged parts of the disintegrating planet. They constructed them in similar ways, but without the earthquake rigs. Dawson

and his team rented twisted tree roots and limbs from a Hollywood company near the Paramount lot. The company loved STAR TREK III: THE SEARCH FOR SPOCK as the movie production team rented their entire stock.

Dawson rigged the stage with explosives. He mixed naphthalene and propane gases to form nap-gas for jetting flames in the earthquake fissures. He also used smoke canisters and mineral oil for other effects. The final shooting employed fourteen men, wind machines and other noise producing equipment. They communicated with hand signals.

One spectacular shot was trimmed from the final cut. It showed Kirk cradling Spock while upheavals tore the Genesis planet apart around them. An immense sun filled the sky, indicating that the planet was careening on a collision course toward its nearby star.

RETURN TO VULCAN

Vulcan appeared different than before. Chris Evans created a stunning matte painting of a Vulcan shrine high atop a craggy cliff top. It wasn't used. A more down-to-earth Vulcan setting was created on a sound stage set with a cyclorama painting as its background. The sequence of the Bird of Prey landing on Vulcan was combined with live footage of actors on the campus of Occidental College in Los Angeles.

Production illustrator Tom Lay designed another Vulcan scene excised from STAR TREK III. The psychically reintegrated Spock would have been taken to the sacred Hall of Ancient Thoughts for part of his recovery rituals. This set would have featured immense heads representing great philosophers and scientific thinkers of Vulcan history. Vast balls of fire would have illuminated the twenty-foot tall sculptures.

Lay admitted that the heads were large photographic cutouts! Scenes on Vulcan were deemed to take up too much screen time so many Vulcan were trimmed from the final cut.

THE WRAP UP

STAR TREK III finished on schedule and under budget, an impressive achievement for a first time film director. Nimoy had picked an experienced crew.

Producer Harve Bennett and director Leonard Nimoy zeroed in on the same theme in the final film: friendship.

Bennett said, "This movie is about honor and friendship and decency and values higher than the complex value system we have inherited since the atomic age. It's a return to innocence."

Nimoy added that the film asks, "What should a person do to help a friend? How deeply should a friendship commitment go? What price should people be willing to pay? What sacrifices, what obstacles will these people endure? That's the emotional line of the film. For me, that's its reason for existence."

The film was released in the summer of 1984. Paramount Studios had another winner. STAR TREK III: THE SEARCH FOR SPOCK was a major triumph.

STAR TREK 4

THE VOYAGE HOME

THE REVIEW

The second, third and fourth STAR TREK films formed a trilogy of loss and redemption. STAR TREK IV: THE VOYAGE HOME headed in a new direction, even if the threatening alien probe seemed reminiscent of STAR TREK: THE MOTION PICTURE. This ode to Greenpeace sent the Enterprise crew on a mission into the past to save the whales when a whale-like alien probe came looking for fellow cetaceans.

The most impressive shot in the film came when the Bird of Prey saved the seagoing mammals from whalers. It created an unspoken comparison between 23rd Century technology and that of the 20th Century.

Amanda missed her son's death and rebirth, but she came back for short yet integral scenes involving Spock regaining his personality. Spock has grown in the feature films.

This film played fast and loose with logic. Characters changed the 20th Century. They even took a 20th century woman back with them, ignoring what her absence will do to the timeline. They don't explain it; they just do it. After all, it's just comedy.

The oddest scene came when Spock swam in the whale tank. Apparently Leonard Nimoy thought so too as he banned stills from this scene.

The movie offered an enjoyable break from grim space battles.

Time travel holds an honored place in science fiction. The popular premise appeared before on STAR TREK. The fourth film combined time travel with humor to excellent effect.

STAR TREK IV: THE VOYAGE HOME

The title, THE VOYAGE HOME, brought reassurance to fans. They needed it after watching Spock die in one film only to be reborn in the next film even as the Enterprise was blown apart. It had been an emotional roller coaster. Harve Bennett and Leonard Nimoy wanted a change of pace. Instead of violence and death they planned to deliver humor and a message that reached out rather than inwards. This was no stranger to the television series

Fans enjoy occasional forays into light comedy. THE VOYAGE HOME delivered effective humor along with an exciting adventure with the fate of the Earth hanging in the balance.

The second through fourth films formed a trilogy. Each film stood on its own, but together they told a complete story resolved in THE VOYAGE HOME. Spock died at the end of THE WRATH OF KHAN to be reborn in THE SEARCH FOR SPOCK. The Vulcan became his old self again in THE VOYAGE HOME.

A TV SENSIBILITY

Harve Bennett brought TV experience to the STAR TREK films. He described STAR TREK II as a classic "bottle show."

"The 'bottle show' in television takes place in an elevator that's hopefully trapped between two floors," he explained. "Or it takes place in a mine shaft where people are desperately coming to try to save you and you have to stay down there and talk a lot.

"Sixty-five percent of the film was on the Enterprise bridge in one incarnation or another. It was also the Reliant bridge. It was also part of the science station. We used that set for sixty-five percent of the movie and that is an incomparable savings in terms of time, dollars and moves. We'd shoot a scene, move

the people out, repaint it and it would be the Reliant."

STAR TREK III: THE SEARCH FOR SPOCK returned to the classic tale of a main character losing his memory. This time it was Spock.

Bennett explained, "You usually do it when your leading actor is exhausted or needs a rest. He's in a coma-like state. In STAR TREK III we had a man who was directing the movie, and who had never directed a feature before, and we felt that to act, and so forth, would kill him. We had our choice of how to utilize that asset. What we did was we spend most of our money building one great set, the Genesis planet, and the story became let's find him while he directs."

THE VOYAGE HOME played on the old TV standby of location. They made it look big by taking it outside the confines of the sound stage.

"How do you go out in the 23rd Century?" Bennett asked. "You come to the 20th Century. The studio asked us how we were going to wardrobe them and Leonard and I said that we were going to wardrobe them just as we left them. 'You're going to have them walking around the streets of San Francisco dressed like that? Who will believe that?' Leonard and I kept assuring them that if we set it up just right, people would believe it."

A MATTER OF TIME

After THE SEARCH FOR SPOCK raked in the cash, Paramount knew they wanted a sequel. Harve Bennett and Leonard Nimoy got together to discuss story ideas a few months later. Eddie Murphy was Paramount's other hot property at the time. Murphy was a STAR TREK fan and wanted to get in the next film. Bennett and Nimoy met with the actor. They discussed their idea of setting the story in the 20th Century. Murphy wanted to see a script.

Steve Meerson and Peter Krikes wrote a script featuring Murphy as a con man. They completed their script in August 1985. Then a new regime came to Paramount. They wisely decided to make more money by keeping STAR TREK and Eddie Murphy separate, getting two films instead of one.

This forced them to approach the script from a fresh point of view. While Meerson and Krikes received screen

THE VOYAGE HOME

credit, Harve Bennett and Nicholas Meyer wrote the final drafts.

THE BAD PROBE

The old Paramount regime had insisted on classic villains in STAR TREK films, partially because they'd been unhappy with STAR TREK: THE MOTION PICTURE. The Earth was again threatened by a giant space probe in THE VOYAGE HOME, but this time for very different reasons.

"The evolution and the freedom of that choice, which resulted from the departure of the old regime, is something that Leonard and I are most proud of," Bennett explained. "It was wonderful to make a movie where there could be danger and suspense and purpose with-

out the twirling of mustaches."

Leonard Nimoy wanted to drop the bad guy approach. He said, "It was not really good STAR TREK to continue to play against a bad guy. Some of our best STAR TREK episodes had no bad guy. We had circumstances, we had problems, we had conditions that we had to deal with, and I felt we should do that now in the films.

DEMANDS OF KIRK

William Shatner delayed and complicated things because of his commitments to the popular weekly T.J. HOOKER series. He also wanted his STAR TREK salary increased. No work on a script could begin as Harve Bennett believed Shatner's absence would kill the series.

Shatner demanded to direct the film. Paramount compromised, agreeing he could direct the fifth STAR TREK film but insisting the studio had already hired Nimoy for STAR TREK IV. Shatner agreed.

Paramount and Shatner had wasted eight months. Bennett and Nimoy finally began work on a new script.

Nimoy said, "We talked at great length about the various possibilities based on the concept that there was a problem in the 23rd Century and that what was needed to solve that problem was lost and could only be found in the 20th Century." Edmund Wilson postulated that the Earth lost ten thousand species per year in the 1990s. It inspired Nimoy.

A WOMAN FOR KIRK

Conducting research led to a new character. Harve Bennett recalled, "I remember saying, well, I know it's corny, but it would be better if it was a woman. Kirk hasn't had a woman to play to, which he does so wonderfully. The whole series is the woman of the week. Remember that whale special we saw where the girl was bidding adieu to the whales who had to leave Marineland because the female was pregnant? They could not keep them and had to send them back to sea and she was bereft. Remember that character? That's the lady, and Leonard thought that was great."

MYSTERY OF MUSIC

One night when Nimoy talked to a friend

THE VOYAGE HOME

about endangered species and humpback whales, he realized the creatures offered what they were looking for. Nimoy recalled, "It had, obviously, the size and it had the mystery and the majesty of these gigantic creatures, and it had the sounds that they make. The signal they put out. We don't really know what that is."

They discussed whether they should translate the whale song in the film, but decided not to. The mystery proved to be more effective. The audience could provide meanings from their imagination.

The producers searched for whale footage, but found little of high caliber. Most footage showed whales swimming away rather than towards the camera, and little was in 35mm. They assembled a team to create the footage.

Most of what is seen in the movie was faked, with only a few shots of real whales. Audience can't tell the difference. Photographers Mark and Debbie Ferrari shot the whale breaching at sea specifically for STAR TREK IV. It was the only real whale seen in the film.

Industrial Light and Magic came aboard in November 1985. Paramount wanted ILM to create magic again. Ken Ralston, visual effects supervisor, and Don Dow, director of effects photography, again led the special effects team. Art Director Nilo Rodis had worked on THE SEARCH FOR SPOCK. He was back again, but this time they also had the artistic expertise of visual consultant Ralph McQuarrie.

McQuarrie had won fame on STAR WARS.

The producers were worried about the whales. An alternate animal would have been substituted if Industrial Light and Magic hadn't found a satisfactory solution. Then synchronicity hit in San Francisco Bay in the form of a lost whale named Humphrey. A few claimed he wasn't lost at all; he knew ILM needed footage. ILM responded to the call. Some people believe ILM didn't win an Oscar for the film because the whale effects looked so real no one knew they were effects.

ON THE SCENE

The news media photographed Humphrey. ILM shot additional whale sequences. At first they planned to shoot only reference footage, but Nimoy wanted something to use in the film, so they shot a lot more. While ILM got good reference material for whale movement and body texture, they couldn't get anything for on screen. Whenever someone approached, the camera-shy whale swam away.

Finally ILM used robotics for the film. No opticals appeared because filming them in the water would have required shooting in real time, particularly since actors appeared. Robotics expert Walt Conti headed the unit. His first radio controlled, self-contained whale proved to be even more ambitious than the mechanical shark Universal built for JAWS in 1974.

The sinking shark on JAWS had become legend. Art director Nilo Rodis feared that Conti couldn't create a realistic whale. Conti delivered brilliantly.

Finding material for the whale's skin that didn't react negatively to immersion for prolonged periods proved difficult. The skin had to remain uniform so that it always looked like the same whale.

The filmmakers, Harve Bennett, Ralph Winter and Leonard Nimoy, wanted it done right. They were willing to risk a new approach to underwater creatures. Conti and ILM opened a new tool chest for directors.

STORM OVER STARFLEET

One impressive special effects scene in STAR TREK IV takes place when the Bird of Prey appears on Vulcan before Kirk and company board it to return to Earth.

Chris Evans supervised the ILM team that created the matte painting. The painting team included Frank Ordaz and Sean Joyce, while the cinematography team consisted of Randy Johnson, Don Dow, Wade Childers and Craig Barron. This shot used a number of elements, including rocks, the sun and the Klingon Bird of Prey model. A blue screen element allowed Amanda and Saavik to appear near the Bird of Prey as it took off.

Matte shots for Starfleet Command on Earth were more complicated. One included a latent image element of live actors interacting with the space shuttle and the Starfleet building! The matte painting of Starfleet was filmed at the Oakland airport on an empty jet runway. Tape markers on the runway showed the actors where they would later be matted into the painting. Objects in the painting were marked as silhouettes on the runway.

A storm ripped through San Francisco near the Golden Gate Bridge when the mysterious space probe wrecked havoc. Jeff Mann of ILM supervised the construction of a sixteen foot long miniature representing half of the full span of the bridge. Dimension was achieved with a forced perspective model. The part closest to the camera was sixteen inches wide while the other end was only two inches wide, creating an illusion of distance.

The storm struck the bridge model in a twenty foot tall, hundred square foot enclosure. The base of the bridge stood in a water tank allowing storm effects. The storm effects were composited against the windows of the Federation Council Chamber so the people inside appeared to witness the havoc. Footage was shot of a real storm striking the Golden Gate Bridge, but it didn't look as dramatic as the ILM effects.

CRAFTING WHALES

Some scenes, including one near the end of the film after the Bird of Prey crash-landed in San Francisco Bay, use full-size mechanical whales on tracks instead of swimming mechanical models breaking the surface and diving again. They could only be used at very specific angles and movements, and weren't flexible enough for underwater sequences.

Conti used the robots in underwater

THE VOYAGE HOME

scenes. He discovered he could obtain realistic movement by keeping the front half of the whale rigid, moving only the tail and pectoral fins. Conti's team built a simple thirty-inch prototype to demonstrate the technique to the studio. The demonstration model moved its tail to swim, but had an umbilical cord coming out of its power source. Paramount was impressed.

ILM hired Pieter Folkens, of the Oceanic Society, to create whale drawings as reference for the technicians and model makers. The artists paid meticulous attention to detail, particularly in the musculature of the tail. The robotics unit was able to design their model so that it looked even more realistic in the water.

Richard Miller sculpted the prototype under the supervision of Pieter Folkens. The four foot long mechanical whale allowed room for servos and radio gear. Tests were run on the tail to learn if it would survive stresses. It couldn't be too thick or the servos wouldn't move the tail. Six weeks of trial and error produced a perfect tail.

SCHOOL FOR WHALES

They built the robotic whale miniature with a three-piece Fiberglas exterior. Making the model watertight proved difficult so each electric servo was sealed instead. Smooth-On manufactured the polyurethane for the skin, making the rigid plastic more pliable by adding a plasticizer.

The model made many individual movements. For example, each fin moved independently in several directions. They were more complicated than the tail that only needed a universal joint pivot controlled by two electrical servos. Microballoons imbedded in the skin provided buoyancy. The whale appeared to move naturally when it swam. Lead weights inside the model kept it upright while moving through the water.

The tail turned the model from right to left, but it needed a small water pump beneath the chin to appear to propel itself through the turns. It added speed to the turns and moved the model up or down.

Underwater sequences weren't filmed at ILM because their water tanks weren't large enough. They were built for tight optical shots involving cloud tanks. Instead ILM filmed

at a nearby high school. Lighting effects were accomplished by filming late in the day as the sun set and light streamed in through the windows. Shafts of light from the setting sun provided depth as it diffracted in the chlorinated water of the pool.

WHALE WRANGLERS

Many people filmed the whale models. Some worked above the water while two worked below. They were called "whale wranglers." Two divers used video cameras to show how everything looked underwater because the film took time to develop and they needed to detect problems immediately. The muddy water contained diatomaceous earth to simulate an ocean and create a sense of scale. The rear of a whale is indistinct against dark ocean water, unlike the head when viewed close up.

They wanted to film the models from below to convey a sense of size. Most whale footage has been shot from the side. Real whales are only seen from certain angles, so the cinematographer wanted to duplicate these angles for realism.

The final sequence occured when the whales, George and Gracie, returned to the 20th Century and were hunted by whalers. Kirk and crew dramatically swoop in to save them and help prevent the crisis in the 23rd Century.

Jeff Mann rigged a forty foot World War II mine sweeper to pass for a whaling vessel. The ship, called the Golden Gate, carried convincing looking harpoon guns on the bow. The harpoon fired in the film is a special effect courtesy of ILM. It bounced off an invisible barrier which turned out to be a gigantic space ship. This effective scene contrasted a 23rd Century vessel with a 20th Century ship at sea.

FULL SCALE WHALE

An impressive scene showed the whales after the Bird of Prey crashlanded in San Francisco Bay. The crew sat on the hull of the partially submerged vessel when the whales broke surface between the cast and the camera. Tests optically added miniature whales, but the producers wanted realism in the shot. The Paramount technicians delivered an effective solution.

Michael Lantieri and Robert Spurlock supervised building full size mechanical whale sections. Entire mechanical whales weren't needed as only sections would be seen emerging from the storm tossed water. The main section, the tail or fluke, was twelve feet wide at the fin and seventeen feet long. There was also a ten foot fin. These full size models look real on film.

A blow hole was used in scenes at the Cetacean Institute when the whale interacted with actors. The model whale skins were manufactured by a contractor, Lance Anderson. Parts of the whale that bent were reinforced with Danskin leotard material and foam rubber to prevent tears. The skins were painstakingly fitted to the Fiberglas shells constructed at Paramount.

The scene with the partially submerged vessel and crew in the water was filmed on the Paramount backlot in an outdoor area lower than the parking lot. It was flooded and blocked off, causing some employees problems when they were told their parking spaces were under water.

Unfortunately, this created a four foot deep tank with six foot high whale sections. A trench was dug six feet deep and twenty by forty feet across to accommodate the model.

William Shatner recently told ENTERTAINMENT TONIGHT about that backlot shooting. He recalled, "I went in there, almost drowned three times, but they said it's great footage! When they saw the rushes, it was all out of focus. (We) had to do it again."

FINISHING THE STORY

Nicholas Meyer came on board at this point of the production. Harve Bennett had written the final draft of THE WRATH OF KHAN with Meyer in ten days. The rewrite of THE VOYAGE HOME was finished in three weeks. Bennett wrote the pre-time travel and post-time travel sequences while Meyer wrote the part of the film set in San Francisco. They rewrote some of each other's sections. Final screen credits give equal weight to the first draft done by Steve Meerson and Peter Krikes.

"Nick always said, 'You know the problem with this script is you've got five endings.' He was right. We did have five endings," Bennett said.

"He said, 'Why don't you have the whales save the earth? That's the end of the picture!' No, I said that's the end of the picture for the hoped for extended audience who's never seen STAR TREK before. For people who have seen STAR TREK before, we have a trilogy to complete. So we've gotta get them back, get them off the hook and give them the Enterprise back. We've got to do that, so that when we finish this picture, we have brought the franchise back to square one and it can go anywhere it wants to go. That's only fair. Besides, that's what the fans want. So that's what we did. We kept every ending."

WATERY LANDING

Originally the alien probe was going to resemble a whale, making its reason for being there more clear cut. ILM first had the probe painted light blue with markings suggestive of barnacles. The coloration changed to black after lighting tests. The probe's antennae, originally immobile, were enlarged and articulated so that they could move. Finally, a shaft of light was added optically in post-production of the sequence.

The main probe model was eight feet long, but a much smaller one was built for long shots. There was also a twenty foot forced perspective model of the probe. This was used to emphasize its size when it descended from the top of the screen. It created an effect similar to the opening shot in STAR WARS.

When the Klingon Bird of Prey landed in San Francisco Bay, it crossed in front of the Golden Gate Bridge while the storm caused by the Probe raged over the area. This was filmed in an enclosed set to allow a driving rain. They filmed live instead of with mattes and opticals to achieve the effect. The Bird of Prey was suspended from a wire rig. Four Bird of Prey models were constructed for this sequence. One was coated with black rubber cement to create the impression of wings singed during its passage through time and entry into Earth's atmosphere.

The models were set on fire when they crash landed in the water. They were also thrown into the water tank. That is why only one survived to be used for THE UNDISCOVERED COUNTRY in 1991.

THE VOYAGE HOME

ENTER THE ENTERPRISE

After Kirk, Spock and the others saved the world, they were rewarded with a brand new Enterprise, the Enterprise-A. They used the model Douglas Trumbull built for STAR TREK: THE MOTION PICTURE in 1979.

It had endured much punishment over the years. By the time it was unpacked for the final scene in THE VOYAGE HOME, it needed slight renovation. ILM's Jeff Man supervised a cleanup team so the model looked pristine and new for its grand unveiling. After all, it was supposed to be a brand new Enterprise. The repairs, detailing and new paint job took two months.

The end of the film is a pleasant surprise. It marked a return of the familiar after galaxy spanning trials and tribulations.

The resurrection was almost as heartfelt as that which marked the return of Mr. Spock.

No major spacecraft models were made other than the probe. They used the Klingon Bird of Prey from THE SEARCH FOR SPOCK. It was now the primary spacecraft used by Kirk and crew. The Reliant from THE WRATH OF KHAN was repainted and called the Saratoga in THE VOYAGE HOME. The shuttle craft Copernicus seen in STAR TREK IV was the model of the Grissom from THE SEARCH FOR SPOCK. Even the shuttle craft Scotty used early in STAR TREK: THE MOTION PICTURE was refurbished and reused in THE VOYAGE HOME.

IMAGINATIVE ILM

The space dock first seen in STAR TREK III was reused on STAR

TREK IV. They reshot the model as no stock footage was used. The space dock was twenty feet in diameter. Its huge network of fibre optics was restored before the reassembled model could be photographed.

ILM did do something new for STAR TREK IV: THE VOYAGE HOME. They created the first moving transporter effect. When Spock walked towards the camera, he beamed up in motion! The motion controlled transporter effect matched the actor's movement. Few people notice the meticulous work. The transporter effect "sparkles" even fade out in conjunction with the movements of Spock.

The STAR TREK film series continued to undo the damage of STAR TREK: THE MOTION PICTURE. The humanistic,

environmentally correct script provided by Nicholas Meyer and Harve Bennett, the work of the actors, and ILM's effects delivered a brilliant STAR TREK IV to theater screens around the world.

ILM again showed they are some of the most talented and imaginative crafts people in the business. Dozens of major films have been brought to life by the facility near San Francisco.

TRANSPARENT LOGIC

Many call the logic of STAR TREK IV slipshod. It breaks the rules of time travel stories. For instance, Scotty gives the formula for transparent aluminum to a 1987 scientist. Bennett said, "There's a wonderful thing in the movie that I didn't agree with, and I was wrong. At the tail-end of the Plexiglas scene, Bones says, 'You realize that by giving him the formula we are altering the future.' Now this is the cardinal rule of all time-travel movies. You're not allowed to alter the future.

"In BACK TO THE FUTURE, given this problem, Christopher Lloyd, playing the mad scientist, says, 'What the hell!' and he goes on and does it. Leonard felt that he had to justify it, hence the scene where Scotty says, 'How do you know we invented the thing?' Which I think, actually, is a charming kind of coda and is also an inside joke to people who make time-travel movies."

Unfortunately that explanation doesn't work. It creates a paradox. Somebody invented it. The formula didn't appear by itself. This

scene alters the future. The person who really invented transparent aluminum has been cheated of his discovery. There is no attempt to discover the inventor although a substance this important would have a known history.

Worse yet is when the U.S. Navy is left with Chekov's communicator after he's captured. A character in the TV episode, "A Piece of the Action," once said the communicator contains the basic technology for many other devices. Apparently the filmmakers felt that comedy permitted carte blanche and negated a need for logic.

TRIBUTE TO REAL HEROES

Paramount originally planned an outlandish premiere for STAR TREK IV in 1984. They considered holding it in Cape Canaveral, Florida. That was before the tragic January 1985 space shuttle disaster. Fans wrote to Paramount asking that the next STAR TREK film pay tribute to the Challenger astronauts.

Harve Bennett recalled, "In the wake of that emotional blow to all of us, we began getting a lot of letters saying, 'Will you recognize the Challenger crew in some way? Could you dedicate this movie to them?' We thought that was more than appropriate. So in the original script, there is a dedication, and it is the dedication that appears at the beginning of the film."

Paramount first felt the dedication was too somber to open a STAR TREK film, particularly one as light-hearted as THE VOYAGE HOME.

The studio also feared critics would accuse them of exploiting the Challenger disaster. Bennett remained adamant in his defense of their intentions.

He insisted, "I said, wait a second! This is not an unrelated event. NASA and STAR TREK are synonymous. Nichelle Nichols worked for ten years after STAR TREK as a recruiter and happened to have recruited Judy Resnick and two other members of that crew. She was really a basket case for two months. They were all friends. The model of the Enterprise is in the Smithsonian Institution. There is a connection between space and STAR TREK that transcends its commercial value. It is symbolic."

The studio insisted on testing the dedication with audiences. The first

THE VOYAGE HOME

test was held in Tucson, Arizona. The crowd was enthusiastic. Paramount wanted to test it again in L.A. with people randomly selected from supermarkets and similar places. They would be given comment cards. This screening, held on the Paramount lot, also went extremely well.

Bennett said, "There was applause, and cards and a question session. In the question session, the group leader asked, 'Was anyone offended by the opening dedication?' One lady got up and said, 'Are you out of your mind?' That was the end of the discussion."

THE FINAL WORD

STAR TREK IV cost $22.5 million to make. It grossed $110 million in the United States alone, proving a STAR TREK film could attract a main-stream audience. It's hard to catch lightning in a bottle twice, someone once observed. What worked once won't necessarily work again because a variety of factors intervene. STAR TREK IV will remain unique.

"In moving through this trilogy," Bennett revealed, "I confess that I used every one of the major tricks I learned in television. I'm out of tricks now, and if there is to be a STAR TREK V, I've gotta find another one because we have now completed a trilogy and we have to go where no man has gone before. When you go where no man has gone before, you have to build things. Then it starts getting expensive." It was the first prediction for STAR TREK V.

STAR TREK 5

THE FINAL FRONTIER

THE REVIEW

Director William Shatner disappointed filmgoers, and Paramount, with STAR TREK V: THE FINAL FRONTIER. His attempts at humor and character development revealed an unhappy truth; he didn't know the characters.

Shatner's script changes made things worse. The newfound half-brother for Spock cut Spock's screen strength in half.

Not all the fault lay with Shatner. Paramount insisted on comedy moments. Scotty got a cheap laugh by banging his head on a bulkhead after trumpeting his knowledge of the new Enterprise. His surprise proclamation of love for Uhura, after two decades of silence, added an awkward moment.

The film cost thirty-two million dollars and grossed only fifty million, less than half the take from THE VOYAGE HOME. They blamed BATMAN, released two weeks later. GHOSTBUSTERS II and the third Indiana Jones film also appeared in the heated summer movie marketplace.

Paramount had slashed the special effects budget, ruining the grand climax. Only a beautiful Klingon Bird of Prey model saved the conclusion.

Bookend scenes of Kirk, Spock and McCoy camping in Yosemite, ending with them singing, "Row, row, row your boat," left something to be desired.

A promotional tag asked why seatbelts were being put in theaters that summer, intended by Paramount to suggest excitement. One writer unflatteringly answered the question by remarking, "To keep the audience from leaving!"

This fumble almost marked the end of the game.

William Shatner finally got his chance to make a
STAR TREK movie. Some of his ideas didn't fly. The
result was a mixed blessing.

STAR TREK V: THE FINAL FRONTIER

The most aptly named TREK film of all was released in June 1989. William Shatner made a deal when he agreed to appear in THE VOYAGE HOME, securing a chance to direct the fifth STAR TREK movie.

Shatner wanted the fifth film to only feature Kirk and Spock. If THE VOYAGE HOME had bombed, Shatner may have persuaded them to drop the supporting players. George Takei complained to friends in the fall of 1986, right before THE VOYAGE HOME opened to the best box office since the first film. Shatner's plan was ignored.

Shatner played down the importance of supporting actors. He still wanted to drop them. In 1989 Shatner told STARLOG, "I've carefully choreographed special moments for everybody into this film. Nobody was ignored. What I've attempted to do in STAR TREK V is to establish relationships between characters that haven't been there before. Scotty and Uhura, for example, are doing something a little bit different this time around. I've taken great pains to have each character do something he or she hasn't done before."

Unfortunately, those "things" revealed how little Shatner understood those characters.

Problems began in production. Nimoy didn't like Shatner's story idea. He didn't want a previously unknown half-brother for Spock. Shatner made some script revisions, but eventually talked Nimoy into accepting his new sibling.

Shatner originally wanted the Enterprise to meet God, who turns out to be the Devil. Co-writer David Loughery told STARLOG, "Paramount liked Bill's outline, but they thought that it was a little too dark. They wanted to make sure that we retained as much humor and fun as possible because they felt that was one of the reasons for the success of THE VOYAGE HOME.

"It really became one of those skull sessions for three weeks where Harve, Bill and I sat in a room and came up with a storyline that Paramount

approved. Then I went ahead and wrote the screenplay, which went through many, many rewrites before it was finished, as these things often do. One particular change was in the character of Sybok. Originally, he was a very messianic, possessed kind of figure who was willing to trample anyone who got in his way, but he began to remind us too much of Khan and we had to take him in a different direction. It would have been easy to write Sybok as a black-hat or a crazed Mohammed, but that was too much like Khan."

CHARACTER INTEGRITY

Nimoy wasn't the only one with misgivings about Shatner's story idea. Everyone forgot to show the story to Gene Roddenberry. Harve

Bennett and Paramount approved the storyline and put David Loughery to work writing the screenplay before Roddenberry knew anything. When he found out, he raised a fuss. Work stopped until Roddenberry could read the outline.

"I created STAR TREK," Roddenberry said. "I don't take anything away from Leonard or Bill or anyone, but I'm the guy who did it. How dare they start something without listening to my comments, whether they follow them or not? I've never insisted they follow them. If I had strong objections to the story, I would have stated them.

"The original story I saw was, 'The Enterprise Meets God.' It had to be even more obvious (that 'God' is an actual alien). I didn't object to an alien claiming to be God, but there was too much in it that an audience could have thought was really God or really the devil. I very strongly resist believing in either. I do not perceive this as a universe that's divided between good and evil. I see it as a universe that is divided between many ideas of what is."

Roddenberry's comments brought changes in Shatner's storyline. "I thought it was very unwise to do a story which seemed to be talking about God because there are so many versions about what God is or isn't," Roddenberry said. "Living in a time in which you have Tammy Bakker and the young lady who got screwed—not that that's an unusual happening in any religion—I think the public was beginning to see that many religions are nothing but film flummery, dedicated to getting as many bucks as possible. I didn't want STAR TREK to be associated with any one of them."

Roddenberry also felt that the story violated the integrity of the characters. He said, "I had some objection to McCoy and the others believing it was God. McCoy was saying, 'Hallelujah, I'm with ya, I'm with ya!' and only Kirk and Spock understood the difference. I said, 'Hey, these are people that have been with you for twenty years, through thick and thin, through a variety of things, and I don't really think you serve them well by having them fall on their face and say, 'I believe, I believe.' I suggested that he [Sybok] better have some power over them if you were going to have

someone like McCoy say, 'I believe.' You'd better have some reason to do it."

Paramount heeded Roddenberry. They gave Sybok the mind-meld power. Roddenberry also said the journey to the center of the universe was impossible because the universe has no center, and Starfleet hadn't explored more than eleven percent of our own galaxy by the 23rd Century.

TALKING TOO FAST

Paramount talked Harve Bennett into returning as producer. He and had clashed with Nimoy during the production of THE VOYAGE HOME. Shatner agreed not to tangle with Bennett if the producer helped develop the screenplay. David

Loughery also worked on the script.

Production on the VOYAGE HOME had been delayed by Shatner's contract negotiations. Nimoy's negotiations also took longer than anticipated. After his success with THREE MEN AND A BABY, Nimoy directed THE GOOD MOTHER. When he finished in 1988 another delay appeared, the Writer's Guild of America strike. Production of THE FINAL FRONTIER began as soon as the strike ended in the fall of 1988.

Filming of STAR TREK V began on October 11, 1988, nearly two years after the release of THE VOYAGE HOME. Shatner hated the delays. The stress began to show.

The first-time movie director was tense. Before this film he'd only directed a few episodes of his TV vehicle T.J. HOOKER. He feared falling in over his head, especially when the first weeks of on-location shooting fared badly. Leonard Nimoy described Shatner's apprehension on the TONIGHT SHOW while promoting the film. He said, "I gave him one piece of advice the first couple of days of shooting. I said, 'Stop talking so fast.' It's the sign of a first-time director. You come on a stage the first day on the set and you're excited and you've got the adrenaline going and you're nervous and if you want to spot a first-time director, you look for the guy with the sweaty palms and he's hyperventilating and he's talking too fast. He thought that by talking fast it would speed up the schedule, but you couldn't understand a word he was saying."

STUDIO PRESSURES

Paramount pressured Shatner to stay on schedule, even when equipment malfunctioned. Shatner recalled, "One of the studio heads came up to me and said, 'If you lose any more time, we're going to have to cut the script.' My initial reaction was anger at being put in that kind of position and, from that point on, I found I was being tugged mentally in two different directions."

Special effects and entire scenes were casually discarded to keep the production on schedule. Other scenes were completed and later dropped.

In the original script, Kirk and Spock's "vacation" sequence intercut with a sequence involving Sulu and Chekov hiking on Mount Rushmore. The gag sequence showed the two officers lost at the base of Mount Rushmore, revealing to the audience that a fifth, female, president had been added to the monument. Preview audiences didn't find it funny. The sequence, one of two by Syd Dutton and Bill Taylor of Illusion Arts, disappeared from the film.

Other problems also vexed Shatner. Extras who worked on the film say Shatner became so upset he knocked off his own toupee. The furious directly sacked all the extras for that day's work when they couldn't refrain from laughing.

The planned $23 million budget increased as production delays mounted. It grew to $32 million, the most expensive TREK film since the first in the series. Six million apiece went to Shatner and Nimoy for acting. That trimmed the thirty-two million to twenty.

Things were pretty slim after paying the director (Shatner) and the rest of the cast.

Unfortunately, Paramount decided not to employ George Lucas' Industrial Light and Magic. They tried to save money by using smaller, less expensive effects houses, and slashed expensive scenes that would have enhanced the film.

Special effects took three months, half the normal time. Producer Ralph Winter did many effects on set to cut post-production opticals. Previous STAR TREK films also did this where possible, such as for the earthquakes on the Genesis planet. Those were later enhanced with optical work.

Ralph Winter turned to Associates and Ferren, the New York-based company run by Bran Ferren,

to produce the effects. Ferren's company had provided the effects for ALTERED STATES, THE MANHATTAN PROJECT, MAKING MR. RIGHT, the musical version of LITTLE SHOP OF HORRORS and other films. Production resources and logistics would be split between New York City and Los Angeles instead of between LA and San Francisco based ILM. Coordinating production on opposite coasts with different time zones proved difficult. Shatner assumed Ralph Winter's liaison role between the production and the special effects house. His lack of experience with special effects led to misunderstandings.

GRAND ENTRANCE

Kirk and Spock first appear on screen in scenes filmed at

Yosemite National Park. Stunt doubles performed the rock climbing sequences, although the usual actors provided establishing shots, including one high on El Capitan. They filmed it at a safe view point then concealed the railing and walkway with a rock facade. It proved necessary to get one shot of Shatner high above ground level.

Glacier Point, three-thousand feet above ground level, offers a panoramic view of the Yosemite Valley. They filmed the shot at this potentially dangerous place. Some tried to talk the director out of it, but he insisted. The cable that secured him to the mountain could hold eight tons.

Pebbles dislodged under Kirk's feet, emphasizing what Spock wryly referred to as "the gravi-ty of [his] situation." Falling rocks would present a danger to climbers and campers below, so they employed easily recovered bound foam pebbles.

Stuntman Ken Bates performed Kirk's fall off the rock face of El Capitan. He wore a safety rig, and set the American distance record for unassisted free falls.

GREAT IDEAS NOT USED

The star and director first conceived a more dramatic opening shot for Kirk on the face of El Capitan. The camera would have started in close-up of him clinging to the rock then slowly pulled back to show the entire Yosemite area. That shot would have cost three hundred and fifty thousand dollars. Instead Shatner filmed against a Fiberglas recreation of the wall of El Capitan painted by Jimmy Betts. It matched the tones of the terrain. Hidden hand holds enabled Shatner to hold on while he performed his dialogue. The Fiberglas wall looked too shiny in some dailies, much to Shatner's dismay.

They filmed Spock's rocket boot-assisted "levitation" by suspending him from a crane arm and shooting him and Shatner from the midsection up. They shot closeups of Shatner and Nimoy at Paramount and Pacific Title optically composited them with a blue screen technique.

A flying Spock rescued Kirk while wearing a different rig with a metal bar attached at his waist. It flipped Nimoy head-over-heels to create his abrupt turnabout pursuing the plummeting Shatner.

Greg Barnett doubled for Nimoy in difficult stunts. Barnett stood in for him during the middle portion of Nimoy's "fall." The stunt man dove off the Fiberglas El Capitan set landing on a strategically placed air bag. Donny Pulford doubled for William Shatner most often in STAR TREK V. He also served Shatner in this capacity on the T.J. HOOKER series. Tom Huff doubled for DeForest Kelley.

They avoided many optical effects by using rear projection for the viewscreen on the Enterprise bridge. Previous films added the images with optical effects after completing filming. The on the set rear projection in this film ran at the same speed as the live shooting to avoid flutter.

THE FINAL FRONTIER

The Enterprise first appeared when Kirk, Spock and McCoy returned in the shuttle from the Earth. Again planned shots were altered or discarded. Bran Ferren originally wanted to show the Enterprise in silhouette against the moon since there wouldn't be a light source. Ralph Winter opposed this idea. He wanted it lit up like a Christmas tree.

Shatner disliked the shot of the motionless Enterprise in front of the moon. He felt it looked fake, like a piece of paper stuck to the moon. They replaced it with a shot of the Enterprise in motion that everyone liked better.

CRASH LANDING

With only three months to complete the special effects, Bran Ferren turned to Peter Wallach Enterprises for assistance. Wallach had previously assisted Ferren on LITTLE SHOP OF HORRORS. They used a converted licorice factory in Hoboken, New Jersey as their studio for complicated motion-control work.

The crash of the shuttle craft Galileo in the Enterprise shuttle bay was the most involved effect Ferren and company created for the film. It looked both spectacular and realistic.

Wanting to avoid the cost of optical effects, they filmed the shuttle craft live, and launched the shuttle craft miniature into the bay at high speed. Normally wires hold such set-ups, but they avoided them because of the explosion. The shuttle crash would have illuminated the wires in 1989. Now common computer techniques erase wires from film.

After considering various methods, including firing the model from an air gun or tilting the set, they launched a sled with two large garage door springs. They overcranked the camera at seventy-two frames for the full frontal shot and at ninety a second for a side view. The crafts men made six plywood models of the shuttle craft but hoped for success within one or two takes to avoid damage.

They photographed the front view of the crash landing behind a bulletproof window. The high speed Panastar camera worked in the same cinemascope, or anamorphic, process as the live action portions of the film. A computer firing chip photoelectrically triggered the pyrotech-nics consisting of twelve separate explosions.

They avoided external trigger wires by placing the firing chip inside the shuttle craft model. Only the trigger mechanism for the thrusters on the shuttle used an attached wire. A circuit with an attached piece of plastic and a monofilament wire led out of the model. When the catapulted model reached the point in its trajectory beyond the length of the wire, the plastic pulled out and closed the circuit, triggering the explosion.

WARP SPEED

The Enterprise entering warp looked like stock footage, but Peter Wallach's crew actually filmed a new scene. After Douglas Trumbull complained about stock footage of his work used in THE WRATH OF KHAN without proper credit, Paramount chose to recreate shots using new footage.

Trumbull's team found that their motion control computer could not effectively "streak" the Enterprise model onto film. It forced them to do the shots by hand, moving the camera down its track one notch at a time. Wallach's team filmed the same way. Bob Lyons, stopwatch in one hand and flashlight in the other, timed each ten-second exposure. Creating the streaking for each single frame was a time-consuming process. Some streaks took fourteen hours to produce. Fortunately the effects team devised a manually operated capping shutter switch.

THE GREAT BARRIER

The great barrier reminded viewers of a similar barrier in the original STAR TREK TV episodes "Where No Man Has Gone Before," "By Any Other Name" and "Is There In Truth No Beauty." It was quite different. This barrier surrounded a planet, the legendary Sha Ka Ree Sybok wrongly believed to be the home of "God."

The script describes the barrier as a huge stellar formation filled with wave fronts caused by explosions in the background. It called for the Enterprise to be swept by waves of radiation as it approached the barrier. They didn't have the money to translate the script to film.

Bran Ferren's crew first tackled the challenge with ultraviolet water dyes. It resulted in an interesting, pulsating, cloud-like effect. The studio found it too violent, although   later

Paramount added lightning bolts and other "violent" effects to the sequence.

The crew also applied the ultraviolet effect to the atmosphere of Sha Ka Ree. They placed clear concentric rings of Plexiglas in a water tank and spun them, creating spiraling currents then injected with ultraviolet dyes and shot with ultraviolet light. It created the required cloud effects. They photographed it with a snorkel lens lowered into the tank. Then a motion controlled camera created the effect of the vessel moving through the roiling clouds.

Ultraviolet dyes were not visible in normal light. Instead they needed a highly concentrated stream of ultraviolet light to photograph the dyes creating the unusual color patterns. They filmed the planet with similar effects shots translated into mattes composited against a star field.

Thunderclouds with pulsating lightning effects for the atmosphere of Sha Ka Ree required a different approach. They affixed balls of cotton to a large flat piece of Plexiglas and shot the 'clouds' from below with a 35mm Arriflex camera. The crew purposely photographed the cotton balls out of focus employing a light source from above. Varying the light intensity generated the look of heat lightning. These effects combined to create the Great Barrier.

SHA KA REE

Live action location shooting for Sha Ka Ree took place in a valley in Trona Peaks, California.

Bran Ferren recreated the look of the terrain as it would appear from the air for the sequence when the Enterprise approached the surface of the planet. Illusion Arts was originally slated to generate these effects.

Director William Shatner found inspiration viewing a retrospective exhibit of Nineteenth Century American landscape painters including Frederic Church, Albert Bierstadt and Thomas Cole, known collectively, along with other artists, as the Hudson Valley School. Shatner hoped to recreate their lush approach on the world of Sha Ka Ree. Instead the incredible shrinking budget changed Sha Ka Ree to a desert world.

Ferren staked new ground by creating the distant barren surface of Sha Ka Ree with a motion control, digital scanning electron microscope. He employed a four-thousand line digital image video processing system combined with high-resolution scanners, transferring the images directly to film stock. Microscopic textures simulated the planet's surface. Ferren tested sand, pollen and other minerals until he scanned a lobster claw left over from lunch. It was the terrain he wanted.

THE DESERT CATHEDRAL

The Stonehenge-type rock structure was filmed as a miniature and a full scale set on the Paramount lot. They constructed and photographed the miniature at the facility in New Jersey, having it emerge from beneath a tabletop representing the planet's surface. Many plaster casts were made of the miniature planet surface to allow multiple takes. Arnie Jacobsen and Jim Bock, the special effects engineers for the rock burst effect, mixed charcoal with the plaster to create geological layers fractured as elevator-propelled shafts of stone shattered the plaster landscape on their way through to the surface. Joe Beymer carpeted portions of the terrain not directly involved in the break-through effect. They filmed at high speeds ranging from seventy-two to ninety-six frames per second.

Paramount originally planned to use makeup effects when the being claiming to be God impersonated images from various religions. Makeup prosthetics artist Kenny Myers sculpted many faces. He included the Greek goddess Hera, an Andorian deity, a Klingon god, and various others, including George Murdock's own classic god image including beard, robes, and all. This last one owed its inspiration to the makeup and costume worn by Charlton Heston as Moses in Cecil B. DeMille's THE TEN COMMANDMENTS.

They found that the make up looked hokey, so they sent the footage to Ferren for optical work. He filmed each head, in varying degrees of transparency, appearing out of a shining red globe (another water-tank effect) and ultimately morphing into actor George Murdock's face.

Viewers found this sequence disappointing. The special effects looked less than impressive. Ferren tried to use a variety of computer imaging techniques.

Ultimately, the entity appeared in a pillar of light (another Biblical reference) using the face of actor George Murdock again. They shot it too late in production. The studio expressed concern that post-production delays would hurt the release date.

Ferren and his crew needed to quickly create the effect. They projected the god-entity on spinning cylinders wrapped in a wrinkled reflective plastic surface. A fog filter on the projectors made the faces appear ethereal. Beam-splitting techniques matched this effect with live-action footage. They enhanced the live-action shoot by using a specially constructed rotating xenon drum emitting a searing twenty-thousand watts of light. Shutters on this device added a pulsating effect that went with the effects footage from Ferren's studio.

Paramount didn't like it! They thought the face looked too realistic. They needed a post-production optical effect, but had to cut corners due to time constraints. The cylinders became the element for the glowing light of "God," but the face shots were combined optically.

Time constraints and budget cuts again destroyed planned scenes. The cuts in the climax left viewers unsatisfied at the end of the film. Shatner endured criticism for STAR TREK V: THE FINAL FRONTIER, but he had objected to the budget cuts.

NOT GOOD ENOUGH

In the planned climax, Sybok wrestled with the entity that adopted his likeness as an explosion left a crater with a huge rock-like being in their steed. It chased Kirk back to the shuttle craft. The only remnant of this in the film appeared as the sound of pounding on the shuttle before Kirk fled out the other end.

Stunt men wearing sixty thousand dollar latex suits had to play rock creatures. Paramount insisted on only one rock man, again scaling down a climactic scene. Rubber suits are notoriously difficult to make convincing. Today it would be done with computer animation, but 1989 was just on the other side of that breakthrough. It would have to be live action.

The latex suit failed on location. It didn't look believable. Short cuts had shortchanged the film. At the time, William Shatner said, "I had the realization that the movie in my head was going to be dif-ferent from the one in reality."

Captain Kirk faces the entity at the end. It is now a globe of light lacking any semblance to George Murdock. It was shot at Paramount on a Fiberglas promontory with a blue screen. A Klingon Bird of Prey was added later. No sooner had The Optical House's Bob Rowholt completed his final compositing than Paramount called him to inform him the sky in the shot was supposed to be black. It had been appearing as various shades of gray. The Optical House traced the problem to mismatched film stock. They fixed the problem by building up contrast. Paramount then changed film stocks, making it necessary to shoot the Bird of Prey again.

Problems plagued the scene. The computer crashed when Robert

THE FINAL FRONTIER

Lyons programmed the new motion control movements for the Bird of Prey. Then the camera monitor broke down. They brazened through with a week left on the post-production deadline.

At last, they had successfully refilmed and composited the Bird of Prey. Then they discovered that the red light used on the set during filming had made it difficult for cameraman Andrew Laszlo to see what he was doing. He hadn't noticed a crewman hiding in the Fiberglas rocks. The crewman appeared in the finished film. Robert Rowholt corrected the problem with a matte, finally bringing this difficult sequence to its bitter end.

BEHIND THE SCENES

Greg Jein had worked on several STAR TREK films and for THE NEXT GENERATION. His shop built the new Bird of Prey for STAR TREK V. The model almost made up for other shortcomings in the special effects of the climax.

Greg Jein built a 20th Century space probe model based on NASA's Pioneer 5. He constructed the six foot long model around a satellite dish. Robert Lyons of Associates and Ferren installed a motor to spin it on its mount. The sequence proved difficult. They planned to have Captain Klaa pilot the Klingon ship, encounter the old Earth probe and blast it to pieces for target practice. Ferren's effects team was quite pleased with their work after trying a number of pyrotechnic and lighting effects. The sequence was dropped for unexplained reasons.

Shatner wanted the final campfire scene in the film to be special. Paramount built a forest set and employed Illusion Arts to create a matte shot showing the grandeur of the park under the stars. Shatner wanted more. He wanted to pull the camera back from the live-action of himself, Leonard Nimoy and DeForest Kelley indulging in an old-fashioned campfire get-together, until their campfire was just a tiny spark seen from miles above. This was inspired by Shatner's viewing of the short film "Powers of Ten," that zooms up from a couple picnicking in a park to a view of the Earth from outer space.

It would have been a monumental undertaking in the time remaining to complete the film. It would have required a number of large matte paintings and flawless dissolves. They toned down the sequence.

Instead they filmed the forest set and campfire from high up in the rafters of the Paramount sound stage in a wide screen process with pine branches in front of the camera. It suggested a view from high up in the forest. The crew matted the footage into a single painting, then combined it with a large star field for the final shot. It also involved simple live animation effects for the river running through the Yosemite Valley. The result measured an impressive four by sixteen feet.

THE END AT LAST

The film completed production on schedule. Paramount hosted a press event to celebrate the December 1988 completion. The principal actors attended in full dress uniform befitting the honored occasion. Paramount Studios hosted the party on the bridge of the Enterprise, featuring green champagne. When pressed for the recipe, a studio official deflected the question by explaining, "It is a secret drink of the mysterious Vulcans."

It marked the conclusion of filming on the fifth STAR TREK motion picture. Asked the secret of STAR TREK's continued success, Shatner replied, "The funny part of it is, none of us know. It is like the cook who goes by taste rather than by recipe. We know the ingredients and we hope they work."

Shatner appeared on CNN's LARRY KING LIVE in June 1989. He explained that he had always wanted to direct, saying, "I have one of those t-shirts—WHAT I REALLY WANT TO DO IS DIRECT. A life-long dream. I've directed a lot of theatre, some television. What you have in front of you is a man who has realized a life-long dream."

Asked what the toughest part of being an actor-director on the film was, Shatner explained, "The two things are totally different. There's the actor who has to be totally concentrated; totally into himself. Totally into the part; the minutia. An actor can be isolated. He can go into his dressing room. He can come rehearse, go away; he does not need to communicate to anybody but his fellow actors at an appropriate time. The director is exactly the opposite. He has to generalize, to communicate with everybody. They're two diametrically opposed jobs and two diametrically opposed personalities."

Shatner's first motion picture directing effort was a very large scale production. When asked whether he needed help, he quite candidly replied, "I needed all the help I could get. I got help from everybody. It is a collaborative art to a certain point. That is, people offer suggestions. Here is another alternate way of doing things; here is a possibility. The director has to adjudicate and then make the selection. It's the director's taste ultimately that arrives on the film."

When asked about the future of the series, James Doohan revealed that he had been signed for a sixth film and that a producer had already been signed for a seventh, but that the box office of STAR TREK V would make the final determination. It took a long time coming. STAR TREK V appeared on June 9, 1989, and Paramount officially announced their plans for STAR TREK VI on November 13, 1990.

STAR TREK V cost $32 million and grossed $50 million in the United States. It's a rare movie that takes in $50 million, yet it grossed less than half of what STAR TREK IV took in. Although the grosses of THE VOYAGE HOME are regarded as unusually high for a STAR TREK film, THE WRATH OF KHAN and THE SEARCH FOR SPOCK each grossed about $80 million. This picture did not achieve STAR TREK box office expectations.

LOOKING BACK

At the time of the release of STAR TREK VI: THE UNDISCOVERED COUNTRY, Shatner looked back on his feature film directing debut. He recognized problems, saying, "We hired a lot of different people. We didn't go after the Lucasfilm people. We went to New York and got other special effects people. So we experimented and I had to learn a great deal, not only about film but about the politics of film on that picture. I don't think I'll make those same errors again."

It didn't discourage Shatner from wanting to direct another movie. He added, "On the contrary. It made me froth with ambition."

Nichelle Nichols has her own views of STAR TREK V. They aren't all bad. She recalled, "I like

five for a lot of reasons, but not nearly as much as four. For a lot of reasons we didn't get the pool of audience. One was the weakness of the script, and another is that we had a lot of competition that year with BATMAN and all the others that came out."

The film created the biggest split in fandom since STAR TREK: THE MOTION PICTURE ten years before. No one knows how posterity will view STAR TREK V: THE FINAL FRONTIER, or how it will fit into the STAR TREK canon. ST: TMP became more accepted as time passed. Perhaps STAR TREK V will also gain acceptance as time goes by.

STAR TREK 6

THE UNDISCOVERED COUNTRY

THE REVIEW

STAR TREK VI: THE UNDISCOVERED COUNTRY told the tale of the Federation-Klingon alliance. The Klingon Empire is part of the Federation in STAR TREK: THE NEXT GENERATION. The germ of this idea began in the first season of the original STAR TREK. The Organians in "Errand of Mercy" predicted a future alliance, something both sides doubted at the time.

The sixth STAR TREK film opened when newly commissioned Captain Sulu of the Excelsior encountered the aftermath of the explosion of Praxis, the main source of power for the Klingon Empire. It quickly led to peace negotiations.

THE UNDISCOVERED COUNTRY presented pure space opera with a bravura Klingon villain played by Christopher Plummer. It was all a conspiracy involving Federation, and even Enterprise, personnel.

They framed Kirk and McCoy for murder and put them on trial in a Klingon court before sentence to an icy prison planet. DeForest Kelley got more than his normal number of good scenes while Spock solved the crime.

The fast paced, dramatic story avoided weak attempts at humor. Except for Sulu, supporting players got little to do. The spotlight remained on Kirk, Spock and McCoy.

Gene Roddenberry objected to less than perfect Starfleet personnel despite the original STAR TREK episode "Balance of Terror" showing a crewman as an outspoken anti-Romulan bigot.

THE UNDISCOVERED COUNTRY brought changes to the STAR TREK universe. Things would never be the same again. They planned the film as the final farewell for the original STAR TREK crew. For most of them, it was.

Fans received a special gift for the silver anniversary of STAR TREK. Many consider it to be the best film in the series.

STAR TREK VI: THE UNDISCOVERED COUNTRY

STAR TREK V: THE FINAL FRONTIER failed to meet expectations in the summer of 1989. Paramount put STAR TREK on the back burner, concentrating on the weekly NEXT GENERATION television series. Then events saved the feature film series.

Paramount knew 1991 marked the 25th anniversary of STAR TREK. A new feature film could boost silver anniversary merchandise sales. They also knew the summer of 1989 had been bad for most movies. BATMAN topped all expectations, earning $250 million, crippling the STAR TREK V and GHOSTBUSTERS II sequels. Paramount decided competition had hurt STAR TREK V, limiting its gross to $50 million instead of the expected $80 or $100 million earned by prior films in the series.

Nimoy co-written and directed STAR TREK IV. Paramount wanted him to repeat his success with STAR TREK VI. Nimoy balked at both starring and directing. He'd tried it once, and only wanted to star again as Spock.

CHOOSING DIRECTIONS

Paramount made Leonard Nimoy the Executive Producer instead. He replaced the departing Harve Bennett. Bennett had wanted to direct the sixth STAR TREK film after his successes with four STAR TREK features. He had revitalized the series after the problems with STAR TREK: THE MOTION PICTURE, controlling costs and scoring box office successes.

Bennett wanted to keep STAR TREK alive by introducing a new cast playing the popular roles, setting the story in the days when Kirk, Spock and the others first met at Starfleet Academy. Bennett's, and David Loughery's, STAR TREK VI exists as a script. The story focuses on young Jim Kirk's development from a careless youth to

a responsible leader, and includes the loss of a great love. The story showed how Kirk and Spock first met and battled slavery on an alien world.

Too many people had a vested interest in doing STAR TREK the old way. The days of the old Enterprise crew at Starfleet Academy may eventually be told in a feature film or new TV series with younger actors, but this wasn't the time.

Paramount, Gene Roddenberry and the regular STAR TREK actors hated the idea. Although studio executive Ned Tanen supported the project, the other studio executives did not. Paramount rejected this approach when Bennett made a make or break demand. He quit the studio when he lost, turning down the offer to produce Paramount's version of STAR TREK VI.

WRITING STAR TREK VI

Nimoy liked Nicholas Meyer's work as co-writer of STAR TREK IV: THE VOYAGE HOME. He asked him to write the new script.

Meanwhile Nimoy became very interested in STAR TREK: THE NEXT GENERATION. He liked the new Klingons at peace with the Federation and wanted to tell the story of the armistice. It formed the basis for STAR TREK VI, the tale of the great peace between two old enemies, the Federation and the Klingon Empire.

These plans predated the sudden fall of the Soviet Union in 1991. Events in the real world paralleled the planned changes for STAR TREK VI. It further justified a story of two old enemies finding peace.

They planned STAR TREK VI as the final film with the original cast and a bridge to THE NEXT GEN-ERATION. It would tell how the Klingons became allies of the Federation. The Enterprise would accom-plish something of far-reaching importance on its final big screen mission.

Denny Martin Flynn and Nicholas Meyer wrote the final draft of STAR TREK VI: THE UNDISCOV-ERED COUNTRY. They turned the finished script in to Paramount in October 1990. Meyer then accepted Paramount's offer to direct the film. Nimoy and Meyer began work in January 1991, in advance of principal photography.

DIRECTING AGAIN

Plans originally called for separate sequences to reintroduce the char-acters one at a time. Audiences would have

THE UNDISCOVERED COUNTRY

met Kirk boarding a flying taxicab, reminiscent of the scene in STAR TREK: THE MOTION PICTURE. Spock would first appear on the Enterprise en route to rescue Kirk and McCoy. Scotty would first be seen giving a lecture in an aircraft hangar while salvaging the Klingon Bird of Prey from STAR TREK IV. They lacked the money for this time consuming prelude.

Other than TIME AFTER TIME and his two STAR TREK films, Meyer's film career has been spotty. Between STAR TREK II and STAR TREK VI Meyer directed three misfires, VOLUNTEERS (a dull comedy starring the otherwise funny Tom Hanks and John Candy), THE DECEIVERS (a 19th Century adventure set in Colonial India starring Pierce Brosnan) and COMPANY BUSINESS (a

Cold War thriller released after the Cold War, two months before STAR TREK VI). STAR TREK VI insured that Meyer will direct again, but his non-science fiction choices have been decidedly unwise.

Paramount and the STAR TREK actors admired the director. DeForest Kelley praised Nicholas Meyer for a variety of talents.

The director finally got to use the title he wanted for STAR TREK II for STAR TREK VI: THE UNDISCOVERED COUNTRY. It was more appropriate for STAR TREK II, taken from Shakespeare's "Hamlet." The famous soliloquy began, "To be or not to be. . ." (Act III, Scene I) and appears in the line, ". . . a weary life, but that dread of something after death, *the undiscovered country* from whose bourn no traveler returns, puzzles the will, and makes us rather to bear those ills we have, than fly to others that we know not of?"

Meyer's and Roddenberry's views of STAR TREK differ. Roddenberry portrayed Starfleet as a pseudo military organization with martial trappings but no aggressive mindset. Meyer views the Enterprise as a future battleship. Uniforms in the first film look as far from martial as possible, but too much like pajamas, Meyer had new uniforms designed for STAR TREK II. They remained, with only minor changes, through STAR TREK VI.

The story of STAR TREK VI shows Kirk following orders he does not support. Kirk's son was slain by Klingons in STAR TREK III. He blames the entire Klingon race. When,

in STAR TREK VI, he is told the Klingons want peace to prevent their death as a race, Kirk says, "Let them die." Shatner played this scene as Kirk making a thoughtless remark he immediately withdrew. Meyer cut the end of the take making Kirk look inflexible, a soldier expressing no compassion for the plight of his enemies.

HIS FIRST SCI FI FILM

Christopher Plummer, one of the finest actors to appear on film, is not commonly linked with science fiction. After hearing Plummer recite dialogue from Shakespeare's "Henry V" on a record, Nicholas Meyer crafted the role of Chang for the actor.

Plummer was born in Canada on December 13,

1927. He began working full time on the stage at the age of 17, maintaining an active stage presence throughout his life. The actor enjoys working in films as well as the stage and will not choose one love over the other. Plummer's early films include STAGE STRUCK (1958), WIND ACROSS THE EVERGLADES (1958) and THE FALL OF THE ROMAN EMPIRE (1964). His most famous film role remains that of the patriarch of the Von Trapp family in THE SOUND OF MUSIC (1965), where he played the romantic lead opposite Julie Andrews. His later films include INSIDE DAISY CLOVER (1965), THE NIGHT OF THE GENERALS (1967), OEDIPUS THE KING (1967), THE ROYAL HUNT OF THE SUN (1969), WATERLOO (1970), THE SPIRAL STAIRCASE (1975), THE MAN WHO WOULD BE KING (1975), THE RETURN OF THE PINK PANTHER (1975) as well as the more recent DRAGNET 1987 (1987), SOUVENIR (1987) and DEADLY SURVEILLANCE (1989). He appeared in the popular 1979 movie MURDER BY DECREE, playing Sherlock Holmes, with James Mason as his Watson.

Christopher Plummer wanted to play a distinctive Klingon. The actor, the director and the makeup team worked together creating the final design. They began by reducing the pronounced bone ridge on his forehead, and added an eye patch to give General Chang a Moshe Dayan look (Dayan was the renowned Israeli military leader of the '60s and '70s). Nilo Rodis bolted the eye patch onto Chang's head. Plummer suggested one of the bolts appear loose, conveying the visual gag of General Chang with a screw loose.

General Chang died a dynamic death with the help of a special mannequin constructed by Steve Jaffe and Ron Roose. The dummy matched the final pose used by the actor.

RETURN OF DAVID WARNER

David Warner plays the Klingon Chancellor Gorkon. He previously appeared in a different role in STAR TREK V: THE FINAL FRONTIER. Nicholas Meyer had worked with Warner in TIME AFTER TIME, one of the actor's finest performances. This time Warner stepped out of his usual role as a villain to deliver a brief but memorable portrayal as the martyred Klingon ambassador. It was a far cry from his part as Jack the Ripper in TIME AFTER TIME.

David Warner's film career playing largely villainous roles began in the 1960s at the age of 22. He appeared in TOM JONES in a supporting role. He occasionally played protagonists as well, appearing in films such as MORGAN (a starring role as a social misfit), STRAW DOGS, THE OMEN (as a photographer beheaded in a bizarre accident), TRON, TIME BANDITS and THE COMPANY OF WOLVES.

THE DARK SIDE

At Nicholas Meyer's suggestion, Margaret Bessara designed Chancellor Gorkon's makeup to be a strange cross between Captain Ahab and Abraham

THE UNDISCOVERED COUNTRY

Lincoln. A strange alliance of forces, including a disturbing faction in the Federation, killed the Chancellor. Gene Roddenberry opposed using these shadowy individuals in the film. The film revealed the assassins of Chancellor Gorkon as Enterprise crewmen. The same pair are seen indulging in racist anti-Klingon remarks. Their presence on the Enterprise negated Roddenberry's concept of a future Earth without prejudice.

Nicholas Meyer felt that bigots would exist among a crew of four hundred. STAR TREK takes place only 300 years in the future, a short period in the history of human development. Roddenberry argued that the world was a far different place three hundred years ago. The people of the 17th

Century were far different from those of the 20th Century.

Clearly many places on Earth in the 20th Century show surprisingly little change. Genocide flares throughout Africa, as well as in Kampuchea (Cambodia) and Bosnia. Ruthless dictatorships rule North Korea, Iraq and Mynamar(Burma). Mothers sell their daughters into slavery in Thailand. The Shoah is less than fifty years old. Sadly some things never change. The human race has not advanced at a uniform rate.

VULCAN MENTOR

Kirstie Alley couldn't reprise her role as Saavik in STAR TREK VI. Meyer changed the character to a Vulcan woman played by Kim Cattrall. Cattrall wanted to make it a new character rather than portray a role already defined by two other actresses. She wanted something fresh.

Cattrall suggested the character be named Lt. Eris, after the Greek goddess of strife, but they wanted something more Vulcan, and chose Valeris. Cattrall disliked the look of previous Vulcan women so Valeris was based on the definitive Vulcan, Spock.

Cattrall explained how she developed her character in the July '92 issue of the bulletin of STAR TREK: THE OFFICIAL FAN CLUB. She said, "Spending a lot of time with Leonard Nimoy is the best way to study the Vulcan culture. He's the history book of Vulcanism. A lot of it he made up—the Vulcan greeting is his, the mind-meld is his—all of this wonderful, imaginative Vulcan behaviorism is his.

So I spent a lot of time with Leonard. We wanted Spock and Valeris to be connected much more than Spock had been connected to any other Vulcan in the series."

Valeris turned out to be part of the murderous conspiracy. It came as a surprise.

The film doesn't explain why she opposed peace with the Klingon Empire, what in the background of this Vulcan woman caused her to betray the Federation and commit murder. The film should have revealed this crucial fact. It left a loose end.

Originally, the actions would have had a reason. They were planned for Saavik. Saavik's love, David Marcus, was killed by Klingons in STAR TREK III: THE SEARCH FOR SPOCK. Saavik may have hated Klingons even though most of those responsible for David's death were killed or imprisoned by the Federation after the destruction of the Genesis planet.

KIM CATTRALL

Born in Liverpool, England in 1957, Kim Cattrall relocated to Canada when she was 11. At the age of 18 she made her film debut in ROSEBUD (1975), playing a young woman kidnapped by Arab terrorists. Peter O'Toole starred in the film. Universal Studios placed her under contract in 1980 after seeing her in a Canadian stage production of "The Rocky Horror Show." The actress appeared on a variety of TV series including QUINCY, COLUMBO and THE PAPER CHASE, and portrayed lead roles in the mini-series SCRUPLES and the TV movie THE GOSSIP COLUMNIST.

Cattrall's subsequent feature film roles include TURK 182, TICKET TO HEAVEN, TRIBUTE, MANNEQUINN, MASQUERADE, MIDNIGHT CROSSING, BONFIRE OF THE VANITIES and BIG TROUBLE IN LITTLE CHINA. She received the most notice for her appearances in the popular PORKY'S film series and the first POLICE ACADEMY movie. After STAR TREK VI she co-starred with Rutger Hauer in the science fiction thriller SPLIT SECOND.

OUTSIDE HELP

Paramount hired small special effects houses to save money on STAR TREK V: THE FINAL FRONTIER. The result ran wild and inconsistent, resulting in a limp ending. The studio chose to return to Industrial Light & Magic, the magicians for STAR TREK II through STAR TREK IV. They brought in Visual Concept Engineering (animation for phasers and transporters), Pacific Data Images (crucial wire removals in zero-gravity sequences) and Cinema Research (for optical work) to help finish on schedule.

Paramount again rigidly controlled the budget, refusing to spend money for new models. They ordered ILM to use those built for previous films. The facility had to repair and restore all the old STAR TREK models. Some had been bounced around for nearly a decade. Internal wiring had to be replaced as it had deteriorated in storage.

The oldest model was the eight foot Enterprise Douglas Trumbull's unit had built for STAR TREK: THE MOTION PICTURE. Industrial Light & Magic never liked this heavy, cumbersome model. They had struggled to manage it for STAR TREK II when Trumbull had refused to help. Now it was back.

It only needed minor refurbishing and new detailing to match the Enterprise-A introduced at the conclusion of STAR TREK IV. The original orbiting space dock first seen in STAR TREK: THE MOTION PICTURE still existed, but only the outer shell could be located. ILM had to reconstruct at least part of the internal section. Budget constraints prevented a total restoration of this model.

BACK FROM THE PAST

ILM got the go-ahead to build one new model, the shuttle craft seen near the beginning of the film. They filmed the approach of the shuttle to the space dock from below, a new angle that avoided the look of stock footage. Stock footage conveys a low budget atmosphere everyone on STAR TREK VI wanted to avoid for the 25th anniversary year.

The Klingon ship model built for STAR TREK: THE MOTION PICTURE reappeared as the Kronos I, Chancellor Gorkon's ship. The originally green model was now white. Model makers Bill George and Mark Moore customized the ship by adding emblems representing victories.

They gave General Chang a more modern Bird of Prey, first seen in STAR TREK III: THE SEARCH FOR SPOCK. The model had previously crash landed in San Francisco Bay for STAR TREK IV. Black rubber cement had been applied to its surface in 1986. When they unpacked the model for the first time in five years, ILM discovered that the rubber cement had hardened as though baked on. It required a thorough cleaning and repainting before it could be filmed again.

SPACE BATTLES

The Excelsior and the Enterprise battled the Bird of Prey of General Chang. Peter Daulton handled motion control for the sequence. The radical movement in the establishing shot swept by the Enterprise from the Bird of Prey's viewpoint. They moved a blue screen behind the Enterprise model to keep it in place. The blue screen had to be moved a hundred and eighty degrees for this shot, a tricky proposition. Only a third of the shot finally appeared on screen.

They found a different look for the photon torpedoes in this film. The torpedoes spun through space with a flare effect surrounding a hot core. Bill George developed the concept at ILM. It gave the photon torpedoes an image reminiscent of the "smart" bombs in the 1990 Gulf War.

The destruction of General Chang's ship involved making a cast of the model in brittle epoxy so that it would shatter easily. They filled the model with miscellaneous parts to hurl out at the moment of destruction. The exploding model was combined with footage of the regular model by filming against a black background, then replacing the motion control

model with a simple lap dissolve. This looked so impressive it was reused in STAR TREK: GENERATIONS.

One unusual sequence combined live action and animation in a startling way for the assassination of Chancellor Gorkon. Many people worked to pull it off. Second unit director Steve Jaff supervised the live action elements. Since Ralph Winter had supervised the filming of a zero gravity sequence in STAR TREK V: THE FINAL FRONTIER, he advised Jaff on how best to make it work. Winter had tipped the set during shooting of a zero gravity scene, reducing the need to digitally erase wires suspending the actors. Surprisingly, blue screen was not used in this sequence, ruled out by the expense. Lighting was more realistic than it would have been. One example is the flashing lantern.

BLOOD IN SPACE

Blood appeared in space for the first time on STAR TREK. Blood droplets drifted through the room in zero gravity using computer animation. Scott Anderson and Liza Scott first tested the bright purple Klingon blood effect. Joe Pasquale and Alex Seiden supervised the final effect.

They developed a computer program displaying drifting, recombining, bubble-like spheres. Jim Mitchell created the stream of blood coming from the first Klingon shot after the assassins board the vessel. Peter Daulton handled the blue screen for the startling sequence of a drifting

severed Klingon arm. No wires were used.

Computer animation added reflections in the floating blood globules based on scanned photos of the sets. Drifting globs of gore cast shadows on the assassins as they walked through a corridor. Joe Pasquale animated computer images to correspond with live-action movements using the precise angles and lighting of the live shot. The shadows were composited in varying degrees of focus depending on location in the picture.

ILM added elements to the sequence, including burning uniforms blasted by phasers and other computer graphics. Paramount didn't want the expensive costumes damaged. Even the rip in Gorkon's uniform is a special effect.

TOOLS OF THE TRADE

Greg Jein's unit had worked on STAR TREK: THE MOTION PICTURE. They returned to work on props, including crafting Chancellor Gorkin's cane with its interesting back story. The cane was carved from the bone of a huge creature Gorkon slew in the distant past. Jein designed the grip to look like a hip bone, while the length of the cane suggested a large fang. Four canes were made, two for David Warner and two light weight ones employed in the zero-gravity sequence.

Jein's outfit also made other Klingon props to float in the zero gravity sequence, including a goblet, laptop computers and a clipboard. They made the laptop computers from molds of the lower half of flying saucers left over from the film BATTERIES NOT INCLUDED.

Greg Jein came up with medical tools for Dr. McCoy. He redressed and painted a Sony eight-millimeter video monitor to represent a Klingon medical monitor. The film displayed a pre-recorded tape during this sequence.

Jein also created the Klingon hand phaser. The movie used holsters from STAR TREK: THE MOTION PICTURE and phasers from STAR TREK II. Jein redesigned the muzzles to fit the holsters. He made other props, including the helmets worn by the inmates of the prison planet. The helmets incorporated designs from the Oakley company, the manufacturers of sunglasses and thermonuclear protection gear.

Scott Snyder, of Greg Jein's shop, built

THE UNDISCOVERED COUNTRY

THE UNDISCOVERED COUNTRY

props used late in the film by Spock and McCoy. The instruments were made with visible built-in lights operated by the actors.

Jein even designed the futuristic rifle carried by the assassin in the climax on Khitomer. He based portions of the futuristic assault rifle on casts from real rifles, but altered and reshaped them for a special Klingon look.

INSIDE JOKES

The technicians sometimes sneaked inside jokes into their work during the long hours and often tedious labor. Designer Nilo Rodis incorporated a reference to a classic television program into the assassination sequence.

The assassins wear Federation space suits for outside work on ships in space. The reflecting face plate was made out of protective eye wear. Rodis included serial numbers on the assassins' helmets. The numbers, E1 02 and E1 11, ostensibly meant Engineering Section One, followed by the crew members number, but E1 02 and E1 11 were also the code numbers for the men from U.N.C.L.E. in the Sixties, Napoleon Solo and Ilya Kuryakin, as portrayed by Robert Vaughn and David McCallum.

Another inside joke turns up on the frozen corpse Kirk and McCoy find on the prison planet. It bears the likeness of make-up supervisor Edward French.

THREE THOUSAND KLINGONS

Budget and time constraints intruded while shooting the Klingon courtroom scene and the prison planet sequence. The Rura Penthe ice world sequences had to be filmed on a large sound stage. Construction of the sets pushed the Klingon courtroom scenes into a smaller sound stage. Originally the Rura Penthe sequences had been slated to be filmed in Alaska, but the expense of location shooting forced them indoors. Production designer Herman Zimmerman saw possibilities rather than drawbacks.

The courtroom scene represented three thousand Klingons observing the trial of James Kirk and Dr. McCoy. Only sixty-five extras were available. They formed three rows of Klingons in the gallery. The rest were represented by a matte painting. The Klingons seen in the most distant reaches of the gallery, as glimpsed in the first establishing shot of the scene, were a miniature set filled with two hundred Worf dolls. These 1/72 scale Worfs moved back and forth through the use of cams attached to motors run by the motion control system. Small Christmas lights suggested the lighted spears.

They filmed the miniature set on its side in a smoke-filled room to get a murky Klingon atmosphere. The crew added live action elements of Kirk and McCoy imprisoned in a pillar of light and actors in Klingon attire in the uppermost tiers with the matte painting of Klingons in the gallery.

A matte painting was also used for the establishing shot of the surface of the planet Rura Penthe. Matte

World created this shot. People walk on the surface of the ice world through the magic of filming extras walking across sheets of white plastic on a San Francisco beach on a cloudy day. They rear-projected the shots onto the matte painting.

Michael Pangrazio of Matte World (an artist who had formerly worked for Industrial Light & Magic) rendered the establishing shot of the planet Khitomer. They combined the painting with two live-action elements, a circular community center in Brandeis, California with extras carrying flags of the planets, and the Fireman's Fund building in Novato, California, featuring a Klingon and a Starfleet officer on a balcony. A man-made lake reflected light in the background. Pangrazio's

painting linked the live action elements by extending the balcony and adding futuristic details to the buildings.

MAKE UP

Eighteen actors portrayed Klingon speaking parts for the trial of Kirk and McCoy, including Michael Dorn as the ancestor of THE NEXT GENERATION's Worf. Close-ups in the gallery required an additional thirty Klingons in full makeup. Forty latex Klingon masks were prepared for medium shots that didn't require detail. Long shots used fifty more simple masks.

Paramount put Marven Westmore in charge of makeup. He bowed out, and selected Michael Mills as his replacement. Ken Myers, known for his work on RETURN OF THE LIVING

DEAD, PART II, served as Mills' assistant. The roles had been reversed in STAR TREK V, with Michael Mills as Ken Meyers's assistant. The two also worked together on the second and third BACK TO THE FUTURE films.

Richard Snell supervised Klingon, Romulan and Vulcan makeup, while Edward French supervised the other aliens seen primarily in the Rura Penthe prison planet sequences. STAR TREK VI featured more aliens than any other film in the series. Twenty main characters required daily specialized makeup. The Rura Penthe sequences, and the final sequence involving the attempted assassination on the Federation President at the peace conference, boosted the daily total to one hundred.

SPOCK AND SAREK

They designed aliens other than Klingons based on the original 1960s television series. Some were slightly revised, but the Romulans, for instance, followed the original design rather than the more stylized version seen on NEXT GENERATION.

Nimoy wanted Spock to look more like the original STAR TREK series, so they lengthened the ears. He wanted Spock to have the slightly sallow skin tone. It required finding a certain type of Max Factor makeup made in the mid- to late-Sixties. They finally matched the vintage skin tone without the makeup.

Sarek appeared for the first time since STAR TREK IV, although his estranged son figured

THE UNDISCOVERED COUNTRY

prominently in STAR TREK V: THE FINAL FRONTIER. Jerry Quist borrowed from THE NEXT GENERATION to refine the Sarek make up, reflecting the original STAR TREK with hints of things to come. The third season NEXT GENERATION episodes "Sarek" and "Unification I" would be broadcast shortly before STAR TREK VI was released.

TWO-FISTED CAPTAIN

Kirk got into a traditional fist-fight, this time with an alien who towered over him. Ed French employed fluorescent makeup so ultraviolet light could trigger changes in coloration. This required the assistance of technicians from the Wildfire company. The same company produced the bizarre makeup effects for Geordi's

transformation into an alien in the NEXT GENERATION episode "Identity Crisis."

Wildfire produces transparent paints sensitive to ultraviolet light. Different shades achieve a variety of effects. Special lighting equipment is required to photograph the effects. Wildfire provided that as well. The equipment can illuminate the special paints from as far away as sixty feet. Nicholas Meyer learned the possibilities of the effects and suggested they increase the intensity of the ultraviolet light to communicate pain.

The defeated creature is an alien bully who has lost more fights than he's won. This was indicated by having the creature's horns look squashed. It didn't communicate well since squashed horns could be normal for an alien.

THE SHAPE-SHIFTER

Martia was an interesting alien shape-shifter played by Iman. The memorable character appeared only in the Rura Penthe sequences. Iman looks exotic without special makeup. They enhanced her natural beauty in a distinctly alien way. Ed French, in close conjunction with hairstylist Jan Alexander, created a wig entirely of feathers. The bird theme went farther. Every bit of hair on Iman, even her eyebrows, was made of small feathers. Iman wore special spotted yellow contact lenses crafted by Richard Snell. He also made contacts for Brent Spiner and Marina Sirtis of THE NEXT GENERATION.

The new process known as Morphing appeared in STAR TREK VI to help Martia shift shapes, as other actors in makeup replaced her image. Martia changed into a brute creature played by Tom Morga and, later, a young girl. It was the first film use of the process on moving characters.

Iman also transformed into Captain Kirk. They digitized film of William Shatner and Iman speaking the same dialogue and precisely morphed the two images.

A BREAKTHROUGH HIT

Everyone loved STAR TREK VI: THE UNDISCOVERED COUNTRY. It grossed $80 million domestically, recapturing the market Paramount feared slipping away after STAR TREK V: THE FINAL FRONTIER. Although peripherally tied into the NEXT GENERATION with the origin of the

THE UNDISCOVERED COUNTRY

Klingon alliance, the movie hedged its bets leaving the door open for another sequel. It still appeared that this was the final flight of the original STAR TREK crew.

The last words heard in STAR TREK VI are a variation of the show's classic introduction, spoken by William Shatner, but altered to pave the way for a new crew by having Shatner say, "To boldly go where no man....or no one...has gone before..."

George Takei, as Captain Sulu, now commanded the Excelsior. He hoped for another film and believed that if the grosses hit $100 million Paramount would release another in '93. Instead the studio held back until the end of the seventh season of NEXT GENERATION. The next STAR TREK film, now primarily featuring THE NEXT GENERATION, appeared in November 1994, three years after THE UNDISCOVERED COUNTRY. They believed the movie marketplace was ready for a new STAR TREK feature film, and they were right.

THE UNDISCOVERED COUNTRY

STAR TREK

GENERATIONS

This film marks the changing of the guard. The Captain is dead; long live the Captain. It may be the last big screen adventure of any of the original STAR TREK crew, but STAR TREK continues.

STAR TREK: GENERATIONS

STAR TREK VI: THE UNDISCOVERED COUNTRY grossed $80 million at the box office, although William Shatner's book STAR TREK MOVIE MEMORIES gives an incorrect figure of $60 million. Not bad for a movie but not equal to STAR TREK II and III and far below the $110 million STAR TREK IV: THE VOYAGE HOME raked in.

George Takei and other original STAR TREK cast members had hoped for $90 to $100 million. It would have assured another film reuniting the entire original cast. $80 million was good, but not good enough. Paramount already had tentative plans for the next STAR TREK film to relaunch the series with the younger cast from the weekly television hit, THE NEXT GENERATION.

Paramount announced the end of the STAR TREK: THE NEXT GENERATION TV series with the seventh season. The smash success was headed for the big screen. Six classic STAR TREK movies had grossed $600 million; THE NEXT GENERATION television series had already taken in more than $500 million. Half of that went directly to Paramount's bottom line. That's not including the merchandising or the sale of 23 million videocassettes.

Paramount wanted to put NEXT GENERATION into the larger arena.

They wanted it ready for Thanksgiving 1994. Plans had begun three years earlier when Brandon Tarticoff was in charge of the studio. Paramount decided it could make more money with THE NEXT GENERATION in feature films instead of a weekly TV series. Season eight actors' salaries and other costs already pushed an ever expanding budget.

PRODUCING THE FUTURE

Rick Berman produced GENERATIONS. He had worked on the NEXT GENERATION since the beginning, when Gene Roddenberry hand picked him as his associate and successor. Berman, a Paramount executive at the time, had not seen

the original STAR TREK series before agreeing to work with Roddenberry. The lowest ranking executive at Paramount had been made liaison because Roddenberry was notoriously difficult to work with. Rick and Gene hit it off from the start, finding much in common.

Berman grew up in New York but attended college at the University of Wisconsin, studying film and television. He wanted to be an actor but got involved in the business end of TV and film instead. He went to work for companies in New York that produced documentaries for such diverse groups as the National Science Foundation, the United States Information Agency and the United Nations.

He won an Emmy as the producer of the children's educational series THE BIG BLUE MARBLE (1977 to 1982), and produced the PBS special THE PRIMAL MIND (1984). His work on this show and other documentaries took him all over the world. When the documentary industry entered a downturn in the early '80s, Berman, his wife and young son relocated to Los Angeles. He landed on his feet at Paramount. Berman began his association with STAR TREK in 1987. He took charge when Gene Roddenberry retired from active participation in 1989.

Berman has been both panned and praised for his handling of Roddenberry's dream child. Majel Barrett, Roddenberry's widow, praises Berman for his handling of the legacy. Barrett told the LOS ANGELES TIMES, "Gene brought Rick down from the white-collar world, in his blue suit and tie, and he taught him STAR TREK. There were all the people who were saying, 'Hey, nobody can do it like Roddenberry,' and that's not true. Rick understands the basic idea, the prime directive, and his main objective is toward a better, kinder, more gentle world."

David Carson directed STAR TREK: GENERATIONS. He also directed episodes of the TV series and the two-hour premiere of DEEP SPACE NINE. Many regard it as the best episode of DS9. His work directing the $12 million DEEP SPACE NINE premiere convinced Paramount that he could handle a feature film.

TWO CHOICES

This time the budget would be $40 million. Time

GENERATIONS

required two scripts to be commissioned at the same time with completely different storylines. The best would go into production. Work began in early 1993, the winner to be chosen by that fall.

Maurice Hurley delivered a story about aliens coming through a rift in space. Captain Picard would turn to holodeck representations of the original STAR TREK crew for advice.

Ron Moore and Brannon Braga conceived the winner. They put a rip in the space-time continuum called the Nexus that forced Picard and Kirk to join forces. Other original STAR TREK crew members appeared early in the film.

THEN THERE WERE THREE

They thought the Big Three, Kirk, Spock

and McCoy, would team up with the crew of the 24th Century Enterprise. Then DeForest Kelley bowed out and Leonard Nimoy turned down what he saw as a secondary role for Spock.

He also turned down directing when Berman insisted there was no time to make the many changes he wanted in the script. Nimoy said he didn't want to come aboard for a project he couldn't fully support.

The first draft of the script had included everyone. Now they excised the missing actors, reducing it to Kirk, Scotty and Chekov, the lighthearted characters.

The scenes written for Kirk, Spock and McCoy had been brief, but classic. One scene put them in a turbolift where Kirk complained that they're regarded as trophies. He said, "That's how they think of us. A collection of trophies they bring out and dust off for special occasions."

McCoy picked up on this, wondering aloud about the inscriptions. He suggested, "Outstanding Starship Captain. Most noted Doctor." Then he glanced at Spock, and continued, "Best Ears."

They eliminated the scene and altered the lines for Spock and McCoy to fit Scotty and Chekov.

Asked whether Kirk meeting Picard was a compromise, Brannon Braga said, "We knew that we wanted the two captains to meet from the get-go, because it was fun and cool. It was not a compromise or a decision that was forced upon us or anything like that. It was the first creative decision that we made about the movie."

Ron Moore added, "We sat down with Rick Berman, the producer of the film, and one of the first things we said was let's put the original cast in. Let's have fun with both generations of STAR TREK, but in the context of it being a NEXT GENERATION movie."

"This is NEXT GENERATION I," Braga said firmly. "This isn't STAR TREK VII." They explained that they chose not to have Q in the movie since he'd just been seen in the final TV episode a few months before the film's release.

If some still called it the last of the original cast films, James Doohan dismissed that assertion. He noted that he and Walter Koenig only appeared in the first twenty minutes of the film. A true transition film should have dealt equally with the two crews. Besides, without Spock, McCoy and the others, they couldn't reunite the original cast.

Walter Koenig and James Doohan were the two cast members most vocal about problems working with William Shatner. Doohan refused to be interviewed for Shatner's 1993 book STAR TREK MEMORIES. Something interesting happened during shared days on the set of GENERATIONS. They became friends instead of only working acquaintances.

Shatner realized it wasn't his movie this time. It was someone else's STAR TREK. In STAR TREK MOVIE MEMORIES, William Shatner told how all of this came to pass, and even published a photo of himself, Koenig and Doohan sitting with hands clasped in friend-

ship, smiling for the camera. Even Walter Koenig admitted to him how unlikely it all was for them to have gotten together like that.

WRITING THE FUTURE

The original cast weren't considered critical for the film, but the main cast members of NEXT GENERATION were. Data played a key part in GENERATIONS yet Brent Spiner refused to sign until his demands were met.

Spiner insisted that in the next 18 months he be offered three non-STAR TREK film scripts to allow his career to continue and grow. Leonard Nimoy did almost the same thing when he signed for STAR TREK III: THE SEARCH FOR SPOCK, getting major roles in the TV movies GOLDA and MARCO

POLO. Spiner knew how fast a career rose or fell in Hollywood and wasn't ready to turn to speaking engagements and book deals for income.

They turned to a classic villain just as in STAR TREK II, III and VI. Soran, an El-Aurian scientist played by Malcolm McDowell, fitted the bill. McDowell let the cat out of the bag months before the film's release, admitting to killing Captain Kirk. Guinan is also an El-Aurian, so the film revealed more about her.

OLD MEETS NEW

Working on a TV series differs from making a motion picture. Patrick Stewart pointed out that films are done more slowly than a one-hour TV series filmed in 8 days.

"Everything, consequently, was able to be done more slowly, more carefully and involved many more rehearsals and takes," Stewart explained. "There was no moving on until everybody involved felt we had gotten it as well as we could. Beyond that, the big thing was that we were able to take the show out of the studio and into some spectacular locations that give the movie an appropriately scenic and epic feeling."

Stewart wanted the original STAR TREK cast, but found himself alone in this desire. "Most of my colleagues didn't share this point of view and felt, since this would be a transitional movie, we should just cut the original cast off," Stewart explained. "I felt having members of the original cast would provide the opportunity to present something really intense and dramatic.

"I was particularly saddened that Leonard and De were not in it. I felt they would have made a marvelous contribution."

TWO CAPTAINS

Patrick Stewart was profoundly grateful that Captain Picard finally met Captain Kirk. He said, "I felt that having the two Captains share screen space was something audiences would enjoy seeing."

In 1987 William Shatner hadn't hidden his resentment of the creation of a new STAR TREK series without him. This conflict reportedly intensified when Shatner blamed the NEXT GENERATION's weekly TV presence for the comparatively soft box-office on STAR TREK V: THE FINAL FRONTIER.

Such misgivings were buried before Shatner joined the project. He and Stewart got to know one another shortly before filming began, during a plane flight between Las Vegas and Los Angeles.

Patrick Stewart recalled, "We talked about our lives, personal things and what STAR TREK had meant to our careers. I was delighted to find out what a sensitive, intelligent and gentle man Bill was. When the time came for us to work together, I felt it would be a good experience, and it was."

Stewart dismissed rumors that he and Shatner suffered a clash of egos and didn't get along during production. Shatner has also disputed those claims. What hasn't been disputed is that Shatner received $5 million more for appearing in

GENERATIONS than Patrick Stewart did.

The first shooting with Shatner and Stewart took place at Whitney Portal. This is in Lone Pine, in the High Sierras a hundred miles north of Los Angeles.

One marvelous bit involved Captain Kirk skydiving. Scotty and Chekov met him on the ground. The scene was, unfortunately, cut from the final version of the film. It would have been the first scene in the movie. The change came so late in the process that publicity stills from this sequence were released before it was cut.

Another scene almost cut was the holodeck sequence filmed on a ship at sea. Director David Carson fought to keep this in because it was an outdoors scene and a diversion from the claustrophobic feeling inside the spacecraft. It opened up the film more, forming a positive transition between the 23rd Century sequence and the 24th Century scenes taking place 78 years later.

THE 24th CENTURY

In September 1994 Jonathan Frakes told the audience of QVC, the home shopping channel, that he was quite happy that he and Michael Dorn, as Worf, have what is called the "B story," or major secondary plotline running through the film. "The film, as big as it is, is a glorified Picard episode," Frakes admitted. "Patrick has the 'A story,' he's the one who the thrust of the story is about.

"The 'B story' is what usually happened on the show. We'd have an away team and Dorn and I would go to Planet Hell and take care of the bad guys, and this is essentially what happens here. Dorn and I are running the away team and we have a good time."

Rivalry between Riker and Worf emerged near the end of season seven. It isn't dealt with in the movie, but may be in future films.

He revealed some other things about the film that perhaps he shouldn't have. He said, "James Kirk does show up, and he doesn't survive, but as we all know, in the STAR TREK world, just because you're dead, doesn't mean you're dead. Ask Denise Crosby.

"The spaceship (the Enterprise) bites the dust. It crashes and, oh, it's awesome! It's big. It's big!"

DORN'S POINT OF VIEW

Michael Dorn appeared on QVC, on October 5, 1994, when STAR TREK: GENERATIONS loomed on the near horizon. The actor discussed the shooting schedule for the film. He reported that they completed filming the final TV episode on April 2, 1994, and started working on the movie on April 11.

He said, "I went right to Hawaii, then came back, and started in. We finished on June 8 or 9." Shortly before his TV appearance, Dorn had been to Paramount to watch the music for the soundtrack of GENERATIONS.

"It was just big," he said. "They had a ninety-four piece orchestra doing this and it was just pretty fantastic. What I saw of it [the movie] on

the little screens was just fantastic."

Dorn also discussed the changes made for the movie. He said, "They redesigned the uniforms, the pins and the Enterprise, and the funny things is, they finally gave me a seat up there behind the horseshoe. I've been standing for seven years and they finally gave me a seat."

He noted that his character's developing relationship with Counselor Troi was not pursued in the movie, but added, "If there is a contract for other movies, you never know. It has been established that we do have some type of relationship. They figured that in the movie there's a lot of things they had to cover. They had to pack a lot of things into this one picture, so that's one of the reasons that they did not pursue the relationship because that's a movie in itself."

ILM ON THE SCENE

Executive producer Bernie Williams and editor Peter Berger had worked on previous STAR TREK features. They brought Industrial Light & Magic back for the special effects. ILM had also worked on the first episode of the TV series. Paramount then switched to other firms because of the comparatively low budget and time constraints of weekly episodic television.

John Knoll is perhaps best known as the original co-creator, with his brother, of Adobe PHOTOSHOP, the leading photo manipulation computer program. He served as the Visual Effects Supervisor on GENERATIONS. When he storyboarded the script to project a budget, he found that they had to make many cuts.

Not much computer animation was done for STAR TREK: GENERATIONS. They used 185 opticals instead.

Model Supervisor John Goodson added detailing to the six foot Enterprise-D model and the Enterprise-B, the reworked ship model seen in STAR TREK III in the space dock sequence. They refurbished the space dock last used in STAR TREK: THE MOTION PICTURE for early scenes in GENERATIONS. ILM saved time and money by using existing models.

They even used the Klingon Bird of Prey model from THE SEARCH FOR SPOCK and THE UNDISCOVERED COUNTRY. They even adopted the spectacular

destruction footage of General Chang's Bird of Prey from STAR TREK VI.

They patterned the photon torpedoes used in the space battle between the Enterprise-D and the Bird of Prey after the effect in STAR TREK: THE MOTION PICTURE. GENERATIONS created their computer graphics based on images from ST: TMP.

DEATH OF THE ENTERPRISE

The most spectacular effect in the film was the crash-landing of the saucer section of the Enterprise-D on the surface of Veridian Three. John Knoll, Bill George and Mark Moore designed this sequence using the official STAR TREK TECHNICAL MANUAL for reference. They made the saucer section

150 feet in height and built a miniature to scale.

They crashed the twelve foot saucer model into a forty by eighty foot miniature landscape of the surface of Veridian Three. The effects men moved the saucer with a post through its middle that fit into a slot in the landscape. The post connected to a small cart to smoothly move forward and back. Two men operated it from underneath the set, maintaining radio contact with the camera crew.

The crashing saucer looked weighty and gigantic because it was shot at 240 frames per second, ten times faster than film is normally photographed. They then projected it at normal speed, shot live on a back-lot, then enhanced the visuals with foreground and background mattes.

The plane crash sequence in ALIVE! provided reference. They learned that a crash scene had to last less than a minute.

BACKGROUND NOISE

Dennis McCarthy, a frequent contributor to NEXT GENERATION and DEEP SPACE NINE, created the musical score. Rick Berman dislikes the rather bombastic orchestral scores heard in previous STAR TREK films. He fires composers for creating that kind of music for THE NEXT GENERATION. Berman wants music to remain in the background at all times, not enhance scenes or heighten drama.

Dennis McCarthy didn't want to reprise NEXT GENERATION episode scores. At a STAR TREK convention in Los Angeles on

October 30, 1994, Brannon Braga was asked whether the music for STAR TREK: GENERATIONS was going to be better than it had been for the TV show. He said that many people complained that the music for the NEXT GENERATION series is somnambulistic, but admitted he had not yet heard the soundtrack for the motion picture.

The original STAR TREK actors began filming on GENERATIONS while the final TV episode of NEXT GENERATION was still in production in March of 1994. The TNG cast switched to STAR TREK: GENERATIONS across the lot the day after they finished work on the season seven finale. Tight schedules created tension on the set.

Just as an early story outline for THE SEARCH FOR SPOCK leaked out a year before that film's release, GENERATIONS suffered a similar blow. An early draft of the screenplay showed up on the Internet. "People are always hungry for details—to the point where scripts disappear from the lot," Kerry McCluggage, chairman of the Paramount Television Group told THE LOS ANGELES TIMES in the November 13th, 1994, edition. The planned death of Kirk became an open secret although it was one Rick Berman and everyone associated with the film refused to discuss.

Berman, now the producer of STAR TREK: GENERATIONS as well as DEEP SPACE NINE and VOYAGER, finds the aggressive fans bewildering. He told the L.A. TIMES, "The people who talk on their computer networks all night long, or the people who go to conventions—it's all a little overwhelming to me. I can't relate that much to people who take this a little bit more seriously than this should be taken."

DESIGNING THE FUTURE

Herman Zimmerman had worked as production designer on THE FINAL FRONTIER and THE UNDISCOVERED COUNTRY. He also came on board for STAR TREK: GENERATIONS, redesigning the bridge on the Enterprise-D, among other tasks. Zimmerman had six months to work on production designs. By then the film had completed eleven weeks of principal photography.

He told the official STAR TREK fan club magazine that the most important new set in the film was Stellar Cartography, a three-story, 30 foot diameter, 300 degree back lighted starfield. It appeared in the scene when Picard and Data tracked the path of the Nexus through space.

Zimmerman said, "Stellar Cartography is dramatic from the point of view of its size and the beauty of the graphics. The scene played in it is, perhaps, the most important single scene in the picture. The discovery and explanation of the force and direction of a complex space phenomenon and how the diabolical scientist, Soran, intends to use it for his dark purposes, is revealed in this scene. It is a high point in the story and we were all pleased with the way the set turned out."

The set cost $110,000 and took eight weeks to build. It appeared on the screen for three minutes.

Another major set, built on location in the Valley of Fire of Nevada, appeared in the climax on the planet Veridian Three. "We spent a very tough four weeks in that environment constructing the necessary settings," Zimmerman explained, "and another two weeks photographing them. The metalwork, frames, ladders, platforms and stairs, as well as all the set dressing and props, were all prefabricated at the Paramount lot and trucked to Nevada, where a helicopter had to be used to get the heaviest pieces to the site."

Filming in the Valley of Fire 65 miles from Las Vegas took place during the summer when temperatures averaged 100 degrees. They climbed a rock face to reach the location. Some days sandstorms forced filming to be canceled.

Zimmerman revealed that they left behind an "artifact" used in the film. Tourists to the area can still see it on a rocky peak.

RUMORS AND RESULTS

An interesting rumor spread during production, saying that Captain Kirk fought against Captain Picard in a duel of starship captains. The origins of the idea remain unknown since it nothing in either script suggests this. They discussed and discarded a similar idea early in the planning stages. No one wanted either Kirk or Picard to appear to be the bad guy.

Other rumors spread when test audiences detected problems in the film in early September and Shatner and others returned to filming. Questions arose as to whether the fate of Kirk had changed.

That question was answered on November 17, 1994, when audiences watched Kirk die when a bridge fell on him rather than being shot in the back by Soran. Other newly added scenes emphasized the teamwork of Kirk and Picard.

Although Paramount downplayed the seriousness of the reshooting, the LOS ANGELES TIMES and ENTERTAINMENT WEEKLY both reported that sources had indicated that Paramount was very concerned over whether STAR TREK: GENERATIONS would perform up to expectations. Three million dollars was spent to make the climax of the film more exciting.

When the LOS ANGELES TIMES asked Berman why that excitement had been missing, he admitted, "It might have been a problem with the writing, or it might have been a problem with the directing or it was probably due to the fact that when we first wrote this movie it was much bigger than we could afford. There were some limitations made to the last sequence that were probably a mistake.

"We storyboarded this movie at five or six days longer than we had, and we had to compress the time. When you have less time to do something, you have to do it less well, especially when you're dealing with action."

The film grew slightly longer, but not better. It is too anticlimactic. The best scenes happen

GENERATIONS

before the unspectacular climax.

Despite this weak ending, the film scored the highest initial weekend box office of any in the STAR TREK series. It raked in $23 million in three days. More big screen outings featuring the cast of STAR TREK: THE NEXT GENERATION will certainly follow.

GENERATIONS

STAR TREK

THE MOVIES: A SUMMARY

THE END OF AN ERA

STAR TREK lie dead and buried fifteen years ago. No new live episode appeared after the TV series perished after a three year run. No one predicted its revitalization and the birth of three related series.

The motion pictures brought new life to STAR TREK. Without them there would be no NEXT GENERATION, DEEP SPACE NINE or VOYAGERS.

STAR TREK: THE MOTION PICTURE worked the miracle. Flaws and all, it restored America's space faring heroes to their adoring public. It appeared on December 7, 1979. Rumors flew that Kirk and crew met God.

The slow, ponderous movie paid too much awestruck reverence to beautiful special effects, giving short shrift to the characters. It was too clinical and dispassionate, too antiseptic to engage the emotions. Home video restored scenes adding life as each character enjoyed a moment in the sun. Spock wept after his mind meld with V'ger.

Leonard Nimoy said, "I think we should say, in deference to the people who made the first STAR TREK motion picture that they had a very special set of problems. For example, there had not been a STAR TREK project for eleven years. We finished making the series in 1968 and here we were in 1979, coming together to do a different STAR TREK project. That meant that a lot of very special circumstances had to be addressed. Ground had to be broken in a special kind of way.

"Do you make comment in the film that eleven years has passed and therefore things have changed? The ship has changed, the uniform has changed, the sets have changed, rank has changed, relationships have changed. We were faced with the concern that we should not be perceived as a blown-up television episode, but should be looked upon as a motion picture. Therefore there were certain changes that were expected by the audience, and they must be addressed."

The pallid movie cost too much. The film went way over budget to make its December release date. One Paramount executive dubbed the production a "thirty-five million dollar turkey," but actual costs made that figure another ten million higher.

Director Robert Wise hated the final cut of the film; Paramount vetoed re-editing. People at the Washington, D.C. premiere reported observing Wise burying his face in his hands, obviously embarrassed. Roddenberry's novelization of the script includes the background information and human interest the film sorely needed.

The video release offers a better STAR TREK: THE MOTION PICTURE, but the film remains a disappointing first big screen appearance for STAR TREK. The film was Gene Roddenberry's brainchild and remained his favorite STAR TREK movie for the rest of his life.

After STAR TREK: THE MOTION PICTURE

packed theaters, no one doubted STAR TREK had an audience. The first film led the way and scored the biggest box office take of any in the series.

GENERATIONS

Fifteen years and seven films later, they dropped the numerical designation for STAR TREK: GENERATIONS. Many things had changed. STAR TREK was now a sure bet and not a chancy proposition. The ailing TV series had become a national institution. No one recalled the original TV series that almost died after two seasons and perished after a third. Now it was a merchandising phenomenon that not only spawned every form of licensing imaginable but three successor series.

STAR TREK: GENERATIONS marked the changing of the guard, the final salute to the original STAR TREK and a hearty piping aboard for THE NEXT GENERATION. Audiences already knew the new crew as the heroes who expanded the STAR TREK mythos in seven years of episodic television, more than twice as long as the life of the classic series.

Rumors accompanied production of the film released on November 17, 1994. It was an open secret that Kirk died, but that overshadowed other elements of the film just as major, including the destruction of the Enterprise-D.

The much ballyhooed return of three of the original cast members filled the first fifteen minutes of screen time in a riveting sequence. They were

END OF AN ERA

aboard the Enterprise-B, the first Enterprise to be commissioned without Captain Kirk at the helm.

The maiden voyage was a press event, with Kirk, Chekov and Scotty along for the ride. Kirk was now legend, but his fate would be decided 78 years later.

The film focused on the characters from the STAR TREK: THE NEXT GENERATION TV series. The story introduced the characters without back stories, assuming the audience knows who they are.

This transition film left much to be desired. It sent the original crew of the Enterprise on their way and introduced the new crew to the big screen, but it did not tell a good story with consistent logic. It seemed the spell struck again. The first NEXT GENERATION film is little better than the first STAR TREK film. Perhaps, like with the other, the films that follow will be far more captivating.